MAGICKA

MAGICKA

Finding Spiritual Guidance
Through Plants, Herbs, Crystals,
and More

CARLOTA SANTOS

ARTISAN | NEW YORK

Library of Congress Cataloging-in-Publication Data is on file.

ISBN 978-1-64829-203-3

Artisan books are available at special discounts when purchased in bulk for premiums and
sales promotions as well as for fundraising or educational use. Special editions or book excerpts
can also be created to specification. For details, please contact special.markets@hbgusa.com.

The publisher is not responsible for websites (or their content) that are not owned by the publisher.

The Hachette Speakers Bureau provides a wide range of authors for speaking events.
To find out more, go to hachettespeakersbureau.com or email HachetteSpeakers@hbgusa.com.

Published by Artisan,
an imprint of Workman Publishing Co., Inc.,
a subsidiary of Hachette Book Group, Inc.
1290 Avenue of the Americas
New York, NY 10104
artisanbooks.com

Artisan is a registered trademark of Workman Publishing Co., Inc.,
a subsidiary of Hachette Book Group, Inc.

Printed in China on responsibly sourced paper
First printing, June 2023
1 3 5 7 9 10 8 6 4 2

How to Read
Magicka

Magicka is a true beginner's guide to help you connect with your energy and all your potential in the magical world. You can also use this book as a reference for looking up specific information. You decide—it's your learning experience.

Contents

MAGICKA

1.
BASIC CONCEPTS

Magic is the energy we each possess to manifest the life we want, to value ourselves, and to live a fuller and more conscious life. There are several types of magic.

White Magic

White magic is performed with good intentions and is used to move our own energy without intervening in the energy of others.

Black Magic

Black magic is used to interfere with the energy of others. It can be used to harm someone or to protect us from someone who has used black magic on us. I believe the latter is the only justifiable reason to use it. A curse, an evil eye, and some types of binding are considered black magic. Some people think there's no distinction between white and black magic and that everything depends on the intention.

Red Magic

Red magic can refer to ancient ritual magic, which is quite complex, or to magic related to sexual energy.

Green Magic

This is one of the oldest magics. It consists of being familiar with natural elements, such as various types of plants, respecting them, and incorporating them into your practice.

Blue Magic

Blue magic uses the element of water in practice.

Pink Magic

This type of magic is similar to red magic, but softer. It's related to love, in its gentler form. Some cultures consider love rituals to be pink magic; others simply consider them white magic.

Witch

The word *witch* can be used to describe women who use magic. It has a historically negative connotation that should be reassessed. Since the second-wave feminist movement of the 1970s, the word has evolved to define women who broke down barriers and obtained the power and freedom that men perceived as a threat. You can practice magic without considering yourself a witch.

Ritual

Although it can be defined in many ways, I see a ritual as a moment where we stop and reflect on a goal or energy that we want to move or find. It can be simple or complex, but the key, in addition to various elements and tools, is to have an intention and trust our intuition.

Intention

Intention is the most important part of a ritual. We can have the most expensive tools, but if we don't have a clear intention, a ritual will not work.

To achieve that intention, we must be calm, clear our minds, and know the goal of our ritual or spell. We must also develop our intuition and connect with our spirituality (some sects call this "opening the third eye," which connects us with the immaterial plane of reality).

Intuition

Intuition is the ability that arises when we connect with our spiritual side and trust our judgment. It's our inner voice that we're not necessarily tuned in to because it's not necessarily a tangible and rational approach to life. But if we can tap into this inner voice, it can provide us with valuable information.

Gift

You don't need a special gift to be in this magical world. All you need is the desire to connect with your spiritual side and start this journey of self-exploration, to reveal what's not visible to the naked eye; you just need the gift of curiosity.

The Freedom in Practicing Magic: Choose What Rings True to You

There are very few rules, and many different sects, when it comes to magic, so you can choose what resonates with you, guided by your intuition.

With the simple act of lighting a candle, looking at the illustrations in a deck of tarot cards, performing a ritual, going outside under the light of the full moon, or gathering with your friends on the solstice, you are already practicing magic by moving energy. When you do it consciously, with intention and self-confidence, you realize the power that wishes, words, and intentions hold, and that's when you discover the full potential of "magical things."

The few rules that do exist come down to the following:

• Focus your rituals and practice on pampering yourself.

• Connect with nature, its seasons, and the phases of the moon.

• Focus your energy on being more conscious, taking better care of yourself, and getting organized.

If you take time to heal your past issues, be self-reflective, and share your magic with others, magic can be a super-powerful tool.

It's also fun. I love the feeling you get after helping a friend with a ritual to get over her shitty ex, or to see things from a different point of view after a tarot session. If you connect with your intuition and trust your connection with the energy of the rituals, cards, or tools you use, you will be amazed at how many things will change. Well-developed intuition, in my opinion, will allow you to see things that have happened or are coming. It helps you feel better about yourself and follow your goals and desires.

What more could you ask for?

2.
MAGIC AROUND THE WORLD

There are various magical practices linked to different cultures. Some are connected to religion, while others are not; some are closed off to outsiders, while others are open.

Closed Practices: Only those who belong to that culture can participate.

Wicca

A neo-pagan religion linked to witchcraft. It was developed in England in the first half of the twentieth century by Gerald Gardner.

Santería

Emerged in the Caribbean through enslaved Africans, who camouflaged their traditional practices with Catholic saints. Recently, it has arrived in Spain through Latin American immigration.

Other Closed Practices: Slavic magic, Roma magic, Pomba Gira, shamanistic magic, voodoo . . .

Kabbalah

Kabbalah has its roots in Judaism. The rituals of this practice are very complex. A traditional kabbalist is called a Mequbbal.

Celtic Magic

Nature and green magic are of great importance in Celtic magic. In Spain, this tradition can be found in Galicia—for example, in the meigas and the water of San Xoan.

Magic is not a religion—it's a series of rituals and traditions to celebrate yourself and nature, to develop your intuition and connect with your spiritual side, the immaterial dimension of reality.

With this book I intend to teach you the basics, the fundamentals, what I do daily.

When incorporating practices from cultures that are not your own, I suggest you ask someone from the culture you want to explore.

The information in this book is open to all, and when I have borrowed something from a specific tradition, I have explained it.

Let's get started.

3.
THE MAGICAL SPACE

The magical space, also called the *altar*, is your personal space.
It's a place for you to connect with your inner self and perform
rituals (such as lighting a candle or incense), put away your stones
and tarot cards, or have a moment of peace and quiet.

Where Do I Set Up My Magical Space?

Your magical space should be in a private area of your home, like a corner of your bedroom. You can add or remove elements to your liking, but it's important that it be a fixed space in the chosen room and that you don't use it for other purposes. This way the energy here will become more powerful and you will feel more connected to it. You can decorate the magical space with items that have special meaning to you or according to the changing seasons (see chapter 7). This is the space where you will perform your rituals, so it's important to clean the energy here regularly. Using protection in your rituals is done simply so that unwanted energies don't intervene, and everything goes well (there's no need to be afraid in this sense). There are many ways to protect a ritual (see pages 20–23). Choose the method that resonates with you.

Protecting Your Magical Space

The first time you set up your altar—once everything is in place—you can do a brief protection ritual. Stand in front of it and think or say:

"This space is sacred to me. I dedicate it to myself, to honor my intuition and inner strength in the company of nature and the elements that I discover in my magical practice."

Then perform one of the protection rituals from the following pages to bless the space.

Intentions and Activating the Elements in Your Magical Space

Each element you add to your altar must be energetically cleansed, activated, and given intention.

First, hold the object (whether it's a tarot card, a stone, or a candle), and then cleanse it (page 64). Then, while holding it, focus all your intention to transmit your energy to it. This will help you achieve your purpose.

Common Altar Layouts

Below is the default layout of my altar (I also like to improvise and add elements that I connect with). In the center, I usually place a tarot card that represents the energy I want to achieve that day or the part of me I want to work on. Also here is the layout of a traditional Wiccan altar, which is more complex.

You don't need all the elements shown below and you may not even recognize some of them (you'll learn more about each one in the following pages). Choose the ones you think you'll need. You can arrange everything to your liking.

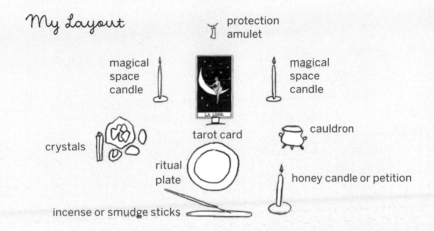

My Layout

protection amulet

magical space candle

magical space candle

tarot card

crystals

cauldron

ritual plate

honey candle or petition

incense or smudge sticks

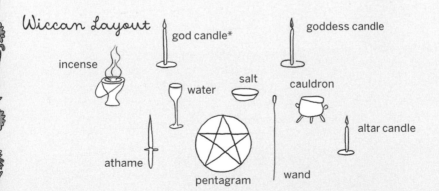

Wiccan Layout

god candle*

goddess candle

incense

water

salt

cauldron

athame

pentagram

wand

altar candle

*The Wiccan god and goddess symbolize the masculine and feminine energies of the universe; since I'm not Wiccan, I don't have them in my magical space.

Ways to Protect your Magical Space

Protection Symbols or Amulets

One of the simplest ways to protect a magical space is to place or draw a symbol of protection above it.

Below, you'll find the most common protective symbols in magic (you'll find detailed information on amulets in chapter 10). Each has its own purpose, and all of them serve as protective elements.

To activate the protective symbol, when you draw it, think of its purpose; if it's an object, think of your intention for it when you hold it in your hands. You can also charge it in the moonlight.

The Pentagram

In addition to being one of the most recognized symbols associated with witches, the pentagram represents the union of all the elements: earth, water, air, fire, and spirit.

The Trisquel

The trisquel symbolizes the balance between body, mind, and spirit and the process of eternal learning.

The Triquetra

The triquetra is a Celtic symbol that represents female power. Each part symbolizes a woman's age: young, mature, and old. It's one of my favorite symbols; the triquetra represents the virtues of each age and the power of unity—united, we are stronger. It's also related to Hecate, Greek goddess of magic, who is often represented with this triple feminine facet.

The Three Moons

Represents the lunar cycle, the menstrual cycle, and, like the triquetra, the ages of women, illustrated with a waxing, full, and waning moon.

The Spiral

Symbolizes the journey of infinite self-knowledge, creation, self-realization, and growth.

The Triskelion

Has a similar meaning to the triquetra, but it incorporates the concept of balance. If there is no balance within and between our three parts (mind, body, and spirit), an overall balance cannot be achieved.

The Sigil

A sigil is a symbol you create yourself with whatever objective you want. (The symbol below is an example of a protection sigil.)

1. Write the sigil's intention.

MY SPACE IS PROTECTED

2. Select the consonants.

MSPCSPRTCTD

3. Get creative and draw a picture with the consonants.

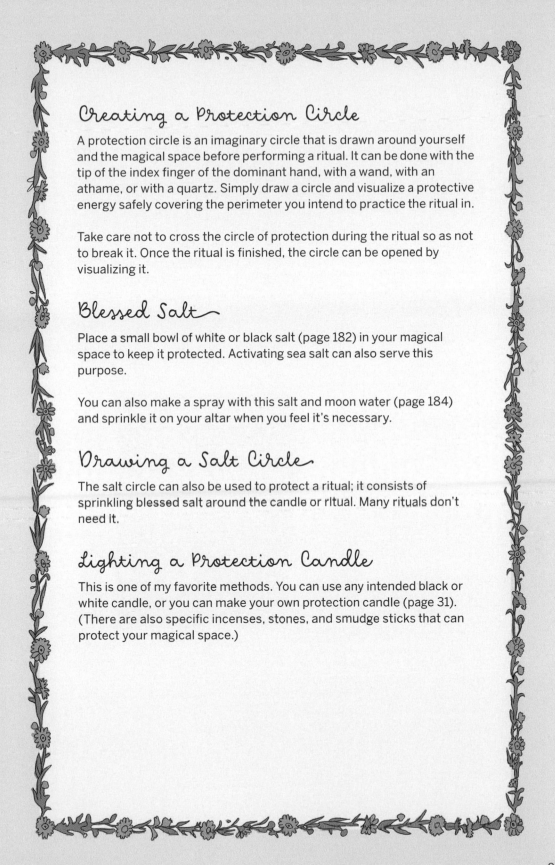

Creating a Protection Circle

A protection circle is an imaginary circle that is drawn around yourself and the magical space before performing a ritual. It can be done with the tip of the index finger of the dominant hand, with a wand, with an athame, or with a quartz. Simply draw a circle and visualize a protective energy safely covering the perimeter you intend to practice the ritual in.

Take care not to cross the circle of protection during the ritual so as not to break it. Once the ritual is finished, the circle can be opened by visualizing it.

Blessed Salt

Place a small bowl of white or black salt (page 182) in your magical space to keep it protected. Activating sea salt can also serve this purpose.

You can also make a spray with this salt and moon water (page 184) and sprinkle it on your altar when you feel it's necessary.

Drawing a Salt Circle

The salt circle can also be used to protect a ritual; it consists of sprinkling blessed salt around the candle or ritual. Many rituals don't need it.

Lighting a Protection Candle

This is one of my favorite methods. You can use any intended black or white candle, or you can make your own protection candle (page 31). (There are also specific incenses, stones, and smudge sticks that can protect your magical space.)

TOOLS

GRIMOIRE

A grimoire is a notebook used to record your magical findings. Preferably, it should be a beautiful notebook so that you keep it as something valuable, and it should have good paper, resistant to the passage of time. Part of my grimoire is in this book, edited as a practical guide for you. A book of shadows is similar, but of a private nature.

Some topics to write down in your grimoire:

- tarot

- astrology

- meaning of candle colors

- dream diary

- properties of different plants

- rituals

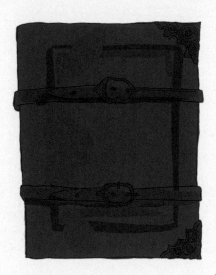

It's advisable to have a calendar or astrological planner to record the most important transits and keep handy the necessary information to perform rituals and manifest at the right time. It's also advisable to have a general sense of the astrological climate and note the phases of the moon.

MAGIC WAND

(OR POWER WAND)

Although it sounds like something out of a Harry Potter story, a magic wand is a tool that helps you channel energy; for example, you can use a wand to draw circles of protection. You can make one yourself or buy one from a craftsperson.

How to Make Your Magic Wand

YOU WILL NEED

- A fallen branch from a tree. Go for a walk in the countryside or in a garden, and when you see a branch of about 4 to 11 inches that speaks to you, ask nature for permission to use it.

- A small quartz for the tip. It can be a rose quartz, an amethyst, a selenite . . . anything that resonates with you. Later in this book (pages 68–75), you'll find the meaning of each stone, in case that helps your decision.

- Natural cotton thread or wire to tie the stone to the tip.

- A knife or athame, or paints (optional). You can decorate your wand to your liking, engraving your name, your zodiac sign, sigils . . . whatever you prefer.

- Feathers, plants, and other decorative elements (optional).

METHOD

Decorate your wand. Then activate, bless, and charge it like any new tool.

ATHAME

An athame is a ceremonial dagger, a type of knife used for magical purposes.

It's mainly used to engrave candles—that is, to write in the candle's wax the words or symbols necessary to perform the ritual. My favorites are the ones with epoxy resin and natural flowers. Athames are usually sold in specialty stores.

You can use a pin to engrave the candles if you don't have an athame.

CAULDRON
(OR CENSER)

A cauldron is one of the most characteristic elements of a witch's aesthetic. It's used to burn herbs and incense. You can also use a burner or another heatproof container; a traditional incense holder is a good investment.

MORTAR

A mortar is used to mix herbs and other elements in different magical recipes.

CANDLEHOLDERS AND PLATES

Choose the candleholders you prefer, but a white plate to perform rituals on is a classic option. It can be a regular dessert plate but should be dedicated only for this purpose.

MATCHES

I always try to have matches in my magical space. Although a candle can be lit with a lighter, it's best to do so with matches or another candle's wick, both to respect the element of fire and per tradition.

JARS, MINI JARS, AND BOTTLES

These jars and bottles are used for making spells and storing different mixtures. Clear glass is best, but it's good to have some opaque glass jars too.

SHELVES AND RACKS

Although the altar's layout is completely up to you, there are craftspeople who make shelves and racks tailored to magical spaces. I find having a shelf helpful for displaying my tarot card of the day. Ideally, the shelf or rack should be made of recycled material or environmentally friendly wood.

CANDLES
The Colors of Candles and Their Meanings

WHITE

Some say that this is the wild-card color, suitable for any ritual; if you don't have a specific color, use a white candle. It's related to purity, innocence, optimism, and cleansing.

BLUE

Transmutation, loyalty, transformation, progress.

GREEN

Abundance, economy, money, hope, fortune, stability.

ORANGE

Peace, entrepreneurship, joy.

YELLOW

Innovation, communication, creativity.

BLACK

Energy cleaning, turning (page 192), protection against negative energies.

RED

Strength, courage, activation, passion, love, sex.

PINK

Romantic love, sweetness, friendship, delicateness.

BROWN

Project consolidation, work, stability.

GOLD

Success, economy, abundance, prosperity.

PURPLE

Spirituality, divination, mental serenity. A purple candle is usually lit during tarot readings.

Types of Candles
According to Their Shape

STANDARD CANDLE

Standard candles are used for rituals. It's best if they're made of organic beeswax or non-GMO soy wax. You can buy them or make them yourself with organic cotton wicks and waxes.

Duration: 1 hour 30 minutes to 2 hours.

SMALL CANDLE

Small candles have the same function as the standard ones. We can use them for shorter rituals or when we have little time to spare.

Duration: 20 to 40 minutes.

TEALIGHT CANDLE

Tealights are small candles that come in a disposable aluminum container. They are short-lived and budget-friendly.

Duration: 30 minutes to 1 hour.

BEESWAX CANDLE

Beeswax candles are made of honeycomb. You can either make them yourself with slices of honeycomb or buy them from craftspeople. They are good for love rituals, but also for a ritual I do twice a month: On the eleventh and twenty-second, light your beeswax candle and wait for the universe to bring you all the good you deserve; meditate on it. The eleventh and twenty-second are master numbers with abounding energy.

Duration: 20 minutes to 1 hour (depending on size).

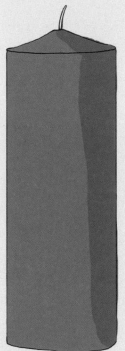

STANDARD PILLAR CANDLE

Pillar candles are generally used for longer and more complex rituals. They are sold in esoteric stores (religious goods stores), but you can also make them yourself with a mold and add different plants or essential oils. Don't leave candles unattended; pillar candles can take several days to burn out.

Duration: 12 to 72 hours.

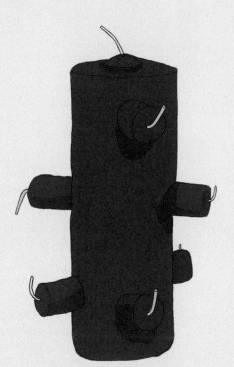

SEVEN-WICK PILLAR CANDLE

This is a very powerful candle. The wicks are lit from the base to the top. It can be used in cleansing rituals or destruction spell work, if, for example, someone has given you an evil eye.

They tend to ignite with a lot of energy, and the interpretation of their remains is important.

Duration: 1 to 20 hours (varies widely).

JAR CANDLES

This is one of my favorite candles, as you can adapt it to your needs. They are fully customizable, and, unlike the previous candles, you can extinguish jar candles whenever you want (always with your fingers or a candle snuffer) and light them when needed.

Nevertheless, in the case of rituals, it's best not to interrupt them; wait for the candles to extinguish on their own. Never leave a candle unattended.

Make your own candle with natural elements. Use natural beeswax or non-GMO soy wax. It's also best to use a wooden wick. Buy a container in your preferred shape or reuse a glass container.

When melting the wax, you can incorporate spices, essential oils, or even glitter. To decorate, you can add stones, dried plants, cinnamon, and other elements to enhance the candle's intention.

To choose the elements that will enhance the candle's intention, turn to pages 68–75 for details on types of stones, and pages 38–57 for details on plant and flower species and their meaning.

To choose the most suitable time to light a candle, see page 122.

HOW TO DRESS A CANDLE

To dress a candle, arrange the different herbs, stones, essential oils, and other elements on a flat surface, slightly heat the candle with the flame of another candle, and roll it over the flat surface.

Interpreting How a Candle Burns

Depending on how a candle burns, we can draw conclusions about how the energy of the ritual is flowing:

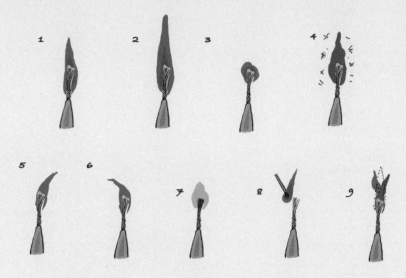

1. **Medium flame:** The ritual is taking place in a favorable way; there are no external energies.

2. **Very high flame:** The ritual will be successful, but be patient.

3. **Weak flame:** The intention is not clear; you have doubts or you are not confident in your ability to perform the ritual successfully.

4. **Noises and sparks when burning:** There are energies or entities intervening in the ritual. There's no reason for them to be negative.

5. **Movement to the right:** Results may come sooner than expected; external energies may be affecting the ritual.

6. **Movement to the left:** Energies from the past may be interfering in the ritual.

7. **Flame that burns out:** The intention is not clear.

8. **Flame that is difficult to light:** You should perform an energy cleanse, or it may not be the right time.

9. **Flame that moves and fluctuates:** Energies foreign to the ritual may be intervening, or your intention is not clear.

Interpreting Wax Residue

By examining the remaining candle wax, we can interpret how the ritual went and what energy is present.

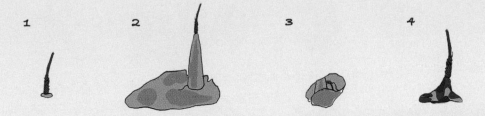

1. **The candle was completely consumed:** The ritual has been a success.

2. **It was not completely consumed because it was extinguished:** The results may come, but difficulties will arise.

3. **The wax choked the candle inward:** The ritual may not have worked, or you may be too anxious and want to see results too quickly.

4. **A lot of soot was produced, and the remains are very dark:** The environment may be energetically charged; I recommend a cleaning.

Ceromancy, the discipline that studies the divinatory meaning of a candle's remains, takes into account the apparent shapes produced by the wax. To see them, you must let your intuition lead you rather than try to rationalize the shapes. Write down the first thing you see without giving it much thought. You should also pay attention to how you're feeling. If you don't like a shape or it doesn't give you a good feeling, trust yourself. If, on the contrary, it seems that the ritual has gone well, trust your judgment.

Some of the most common interpretations of candle wax shapes are as follows (but remember to listen to your intuition).

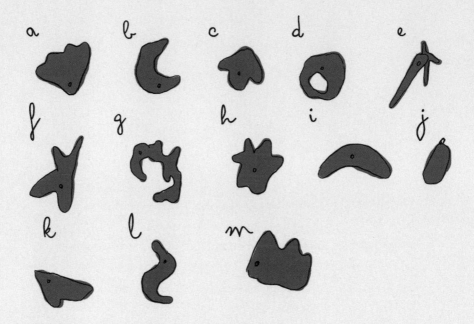

a. **Fan:** possibilities and surprises.

b. **Moon:** worries, well-being issues.

c. **Bee:** luck, good beginnings.

d. **Ring:** good economy, commitments.

e. **Needle:** hazards.

f. **Scissors:** separations, breakups, lovesickness.

g. **Chains:** long-lasting union.

h. **Sun or star:** good luck.

i. **Bridge:** time to start or to take a risk.

j. **Candle:** connection with our spiritual part.

k. **Airplane:** travel, change of phase, surprise.

l. **Snake:** possible betrayal or disappointment.

m. **Mountains:** obstacles, but also strength.

4.
HERBARIUM

The Use of Plants in Magic

- How to grow your own magical garden.
- How to use botanicals in magic.
- Smudge sticks.
- Essential oils.

HERBARIUM

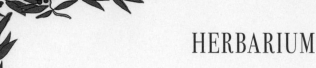

How to Grow Your Own Magical Garden

It's important that you establish a relationship with your herbs and plants so that your rituals have greater strength. Ideally, your magical garden should include your favorite plants so that you want to take care of them and establish a connection. Have you ever heard that if you talk to plants, they grow better and stronger? In magic, it's important to pamper them, and to ask them and nature for permission to use them so that you can work together. You can use them fresh or dried. If you don't have a space where you can grow and care for your own plants, you can buy them already dried from an herbalist's shop and transfer your energy to them.

To dry a plant: Ask the plant's permission to cut it. Lay the plant on a paper towel or cloth to allow for any moisture to evaporate. Next, tie it by the stem to a natural branch and hang it upside down in a dry place. Drying will take more or less time depending on the type of plant; just keep your eye on it. Once they are dried, you can store plants in glass jars and label them or grind them with your mortar and use them as incense, in bath salts, or in candles.

How to Use Herbs

To decorate your magical space

You can use herbs dried or fresh as decoration for your altar or magical space. In chapter 7 you'll learn more about which plants and other elements are associated with each magical festivity and, therefore, with each season of the year.

As incense

While it's fine to have classic incense sticks or cones, you can also use dried plants by burning them in an incense burner or in your cauldron. For this you will need a charcoal burner, matches, and a ventilated space. Do not use fresh herbs for this; they must be dried. You can grind them in a mortar or light them as is (remember, matches are preferred).

As teas or infusions

You should check that the plant you are going to infuse is not toxic, or just buy the infusions directly from specialized stores. On pages 58–59 you will find details on plants to use for making tea and how to ritualize your morning tea or coffee by giving it intention.

As bath salts

On page 182 you will find a variety of salts that you can combine with plants and essential oils for ritual baths with different intentions. My favorite is the Aphrodite bath salts designed to attract love and self-esteem (page 188).

As smudge sticks

Smudge sticks are herb bundles that serve different purposes. You can make them yourself by drying fresh herbs tied together in bundles instead of hanging them, or you can buy them ready-made. You can use different types of plants or branches, such as palo santo, cinnamon, or sandalwood, for smudge; you'll find a summary of the most common ones on pages 60–61.

As essential oils or extracts

On page 62 you will find a summary of how to incorporate them into your practice. I buy them ready-made at specialized stores.

BAY LEAF
(Laurus nobilis)

GENDER: Male
ELEMENT: Fire
PLANET: Sun
ORIGIN: Mediterranean

MEDICINAL PROPERTIES:
Relieves indigestion, migraines, gas, and colds.

NOTE:
In some cultures, the bay leaf from a stew is placed on a single woman's plate to help her find a boyfriend.

The bay leaf also symbolizes success, which is why conquerors and emperors were crowned with bay leaves, aka laurels, in ancient Rome. This is where the word *laureate* comes from.

MAGICAL PROPERTIES:
Since ancient times, the bay leaf has been considered protective and purifying. It's used against negative energies; in protection rituals it's a great alternative to palo santo or white sage.

It's also associated with good fortune, luck, and success and used in related rituals.

As an amulet, it's often placed on a house's doors for protection.

RITUALS:
On the new moon, write a simple wish with gold ink on a bay leaf (tranquility, love, inspiration . . .) and burn it, asking the moon to fulfill it.

Put a bay leaf under your pillow to help awaken your psychic abilities.

Burn a bay leaf to cleanse the energy in your home, then throw the ashes out the window.

ROSEMARY
(Salvia rosmarinus)

GENDER: Male
ELEMENT: Fire
PLANETS: Sun, Venus
ORIGIN: Mediterranean

MEDICINAL PROPERTIES:
Helps with memory and sleep; relieves muscle pain.

NOTE:
In ancient Greece, students would place rosemary branches on their heads to stimulate their memory.

MAGICAL PROPERTIES:
Rosemary is associated with protection, luck in love, friendship, and loyalty and used in related rituals.

POPPY
(Papaver rhoeas)

GENDER: Female
ELEMENT: Water
PLANET: Moon
ORIGIN: Eurasia, northern Africa

MAGICAL PROPERTIES:
The poppy is associated with themes related to the moon: love, dreams, spirituality, fertility.

Some deities associated with the poppy are Demeter, Aphrodite, Selene, and Nyx.

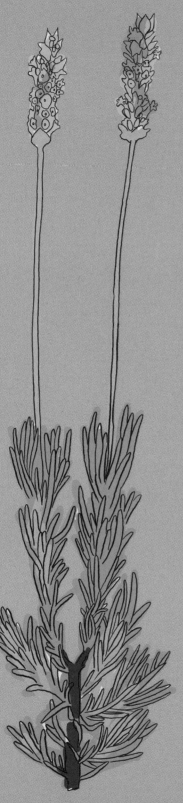

LAVENDER
(Lavandula angustifolia)

GENDER: Male
ELEMENT: Air
PLANET: Mercury
ORIGIN: Europe

MEDICINAL PROPERTIES:
Painkiller, antibacterial, and antiseptic.

MAGICAL PROPERTIES:
It's associated with aphrodisiacs, sex, love, harmony, happiness, virility, peace, and secrets and is used in rituals with these themes.

One of my favorite ways to use lavender is mixing it with salt for a relaxing bath. This helps break up blockages and cleanse. It's used in rituals to increase self-esteem (see recipe on page 188). It's a versatile plant, and in many rituals it can often replace other plants that are harder to find.

It's common to keep a white bag with dried lavender under your pillow to help you fall asleep and attract positive energies. It's also a good protector and sweetener in situations of love.

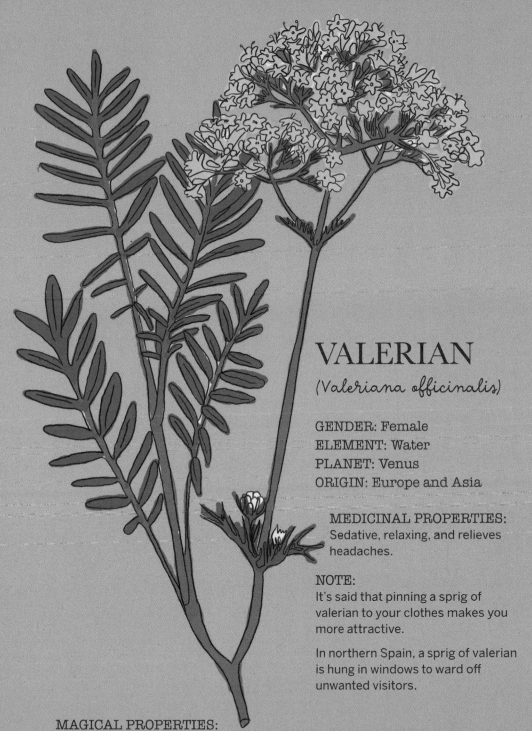

VALERIAN
(Valeriana officinalis)

GENDER: Female
ELEMENT: Water
PLANET: Venus
ORIGIN: Europe and Asia

MEDICINAL PROPERTIES:
Sedative, relaxing, and relieves headaches.

NOTE:
It's said that pinning a sprig of valerian to your clothes makes you more attractive.

In northern Spain, a sprig of valerian is hung in windows to ward off unwanted visitors.

MAGICAL PROPERTIES:
Valerian is used in beauty and protection rituals. Since it's related to Venus and the goddess Aphrodite, valerian has a very important use in rituals related to seeing our own beauty, and to feeling comfortable and happy with ourselves.

WHITE SAGE
(Salvia apiana)

GENDER: Male
ELEMENT: Air
PLANET: Jupiter
ORIGIN: Southern California and Mexico

MEDICINAL PROPERTIES:
Soothing and relaxing; widely used in natural medicine.

MAGICAL PROPERTIES:
White sage, and in particular bundles or smudge sticks of white sage, is one of the most commonly used plants for cleansing and other rituals in many cultures.

Some Indigenous peoples with ties to the plant's native range consider white sage sacred, so there is some controversy as to whether it's cultural appropriation to use this plant in magical practice.

Other plants can also be used for cleansing, such as rosemary, bay leaf, or other varieties of sage. In order to select the proper plant, it's best to listen to the opinion of Indigenous people and to proceed consciously.

See how to make herb bundles on pages 60–61.

RITUAL:
On a piece of paper, write about or draw a picture of something you want to get rid of (for example, doubts or insecurity) and burn some sage every night until, little by little, it's gone.

DANDELION
(Taraxacum officinale)

GENDER: Female
ELEMENT: Water
PLANET: Jupiter
ORIGIN: Europe and Asia

MEDICINAL PROPERTIES:
Diuretic, lowers blood pressure, fungicide, and bactericide.

MAGICAL PROPERTIES:
Dandelion is associated with fairies. Traditionally, one should make a wish when blowing a dandelion. It's used in rituals of luck, love, and destiny.

CHAMOMILE
(Chamaemelum nobile)

GENDER: Female
ELEMENT: Water
PLANET: Sun
ORIGIN: Europe

MEDICINAL PROPERTIES:
Calming and relaxing; relieves stomach problems.

MAGICAL PROPERTIES:
It's used as an oracle to find out whether your love for someone is reciprocated. Tear the petals off one by one in a game of "They love me, they love me not," until only one petal is left. It's used in rituals to attract abundance, money, or love.

STAR ANISE
(Illicium verum)

GENDER: Male
ELEMENT: Air
PLANET: Mercury/Jupiter
ORIGIN: Southeast China and Vietnam

MEDICINAL PROPERTIES:
Stimulant, diuretic, expectorant. Combats colds, flus, and congestion.

MAGICAL PROPERTIES:
Star anise connects us to our spiritual side, and it's said to help us be more in tune with other planes of our reality.

It's also very important for spiritual protection, preventing unrelated energies from intervening in our rituals.

Anise fruit is often used in protection and astral projection rituals (the latter are very complicated to perform and are not recommended).

RITUAL:
Place a star anise in each corner of your altar (symbolizing the four elements: air, earth, water, and fire) to give protection and strength to your rituals.

Star anise is also used in rituals of protection and for spiritual and psychic development.

JUNIPER
(Juniperus communis)

GENDER: Male
ELEMENT: Fire
PLANET: Sun
ORIGIN: Europe, North America, and Asia

MEDICINAL PROPERTIES:
Digestive, soothing, treats urinary tract infections, bactericide, and fungicide.

MAGICAL PROPERTIES:
It's often used in purification rituals, especially in the form of essential oil. You can also protect your altar with juniper branches or berries.

VANILLA
(Vanilla spp.)

GENDER: Female
ELEMENT: Water
PLANET: Venus
ORIGIN: Central and South America

MEDICINAL PROPERTIES:
Strengthens hair, anti-inflammatory, and prevents acne.

MAGICAL PROPERTIES:
It's often used in baths and rituals of abundance and prosperity, as well as in rituals to sweeten a situation or relationship.

It's a frequent element in love spells, especially when you want to attract a person with masculine or yang energy.

ROSE

(Rosa spp.)

GENDER: Female
ELEMENT: Water
PLANET: Venus
ORIGIN: Europe,
North America,
and Asia

There are many
types of roses. Use the
candle colors on page 28
to help guide you on what
each color of this flower
means.

MEDICINAL PROPERTIES:

Rose water and rose
hip oil are widely used
for nourishing the skin
and in remedies to
strengthen hair.

MAGICAL PROPERTIES:

The rose is associated with
beauty and love in many
cultures. Both its petals and
its essential oil are often
used in related rituals.

It's also used in rituals to
inspire peace of mind,
tranquility, commitment, and
emotional healing.

It's a perfect element for decorating
your altar in the spring.

TARRAGON

(Artemisia dracunculus)

GENDER: Male
ELEMENT: Fire
PLANET: Sun
ORIGIN: Europe (Scandinavia), Asia,
and North America

MEDICINAL PROPERTIES:
Relieves digestive and menstrual problems,
toothaches, and fluid retention.

MAGICAL PROPERTIES:
It's often used in rituals of attraction and
manifestation.

BASIL

(Ocimum basilicum)

GENDER: Male
ELEMENT: Fire
PLANET: Mars
ORIGIN: Southern Asia and Australia

MEDICINAL PROPERTIES:
Helps with gastrointestinal problems.

MAGICAL PROPERTIES:
Basil is often used in rituals related to fertility, sexual
attraction, and economic prosperity.

It's also used to help us achieve our goals, especially when it
comes to career success, and to strengthen our willpower.

PEPPER

(Piper spp.)

GENDER: Male
ELEMENT: Fire
PLANET: Mars
ORIGIN: India

MEDICINAL PROPERTIES:
Anti-inflammatory, antiseptic, and helps treat respiratory issues.

MAGICAL PROPERTIES:
Although it has several uses, one of the most popular is as an accelerator or to unblock situations that are at a standstill. It's also associated with sex and attraction.

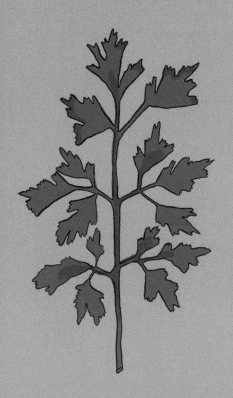

PARSLEY

(Petroselinum crispum)

GENDER: Male
ELEMENT: Earth
PLANET: Mercury
ORIGIN: Europe and the Mediterranean

MEDICINAL PROPERTIES:
Diuretic, anticoagulant, and prevents anemia.

MAGICAL PROPERTIES:
It balances energies, and it also functions as a space cleanser.

GARLIC
(Allium sativum)

GENDER: Male
ELEMENT: Fire
PLANET: Mars
ORIGIN: Central Asia

MEDICINAL PROPERTIES:
Lowers cholesterol, relieves colds, and supports the immune system.

MAGICAL PROPERTIES:
Often used in protection rituals, in particular for gaining courage, bravery, and self-esteem.

It's also used to break spells and curses.

It's a frequent element in both white and black magic.

MINT

(Mentha spp.)

GENDER: Female
ELEMENT: Air
PLANET: Mercury
ORIGIN: Global

MEDICINAL PROPERTIES:
Anti-inflammatory, antiseptic, and helps treat respiratory issues.

MAGICAL PROPERTIES:
It's used for prosperity and protection, especially in travel.

Pour peppermint oil on the threshold of your home to attract good luck.

Mint is associated with the goddess Hecate.

STRAWBERRY

(Fragaria spp.)

GENDER: Female
ELEMENT: Earth
PLANET: Venus
ORIGIN: Global

MEDICINAL PROPERTIES:
Helps whiten teeth and clear up skin; used as an exfoliator and acne preventer.

MAGICAL PROPERTIES:
It's usually related to love, rituals of self-love, and attraction to a person (especially male).

RASPBERRY
(Rubus idaeus)

GENDER: Female
ELEMENT: Water
PLANET: Venus
ORIGIN: Europe and North America

MEDICINAL PROPERTIES:
Antioxidant and promotes healthy skin.

MAGICAL PROPERTIES:
The branches of this plant are hung on windows for protection.

It's related to love, childbirth, and motherhood. It can be used in rituals directly or indirectly connected to these themes.

CLOVE
(Syzygium aromaticum)

GENDER: Male
ELEMENT: Earth
PLANET: Mercury
ORIGIN: Indonesia

MEDICINAL PROPERTIES:
Antiseptic, stimulant, digestive, and disinfectant.

MAGICAL PROPERTIES:
It's related to protection, purification, love, lust, and energy cleansing.

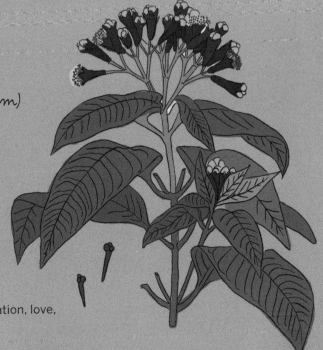

PATCHOULI

(Pogostemon cablin)

GENDER: Female
ELEMENT: Earth
PLANET: Saturn
ORIGIN: Indonesia

MEDICINAL PROPERTIES:
Antiseptic, aphrodisiac, astringent, and deodorant.

MAGICAL PROPERTIES:
It's often used in rituals related to economic prosperity (money, business, economy, abundance) and in rituals for sensuality and protection, but this is less frequent.

SANDALWOOD

(Santalum album)

GENDER: Male
ELEMENT: Earth
PLANET: Mercury
ORIGIN: Southeast Asia, Australia, islands of the South Pacific

(It's usually sold as a twig, as shown here.)

MEDICINAL PROPERTIES:
Promotes healthy and good-looking skin; anti-inflammatory.

MAGICAL PROPERTIES:
It's often used in love rituals and to attract beings of light to help us in our rituals.

PALO SANTO

(Bursera graveolens)

GENDER: Female
ELEMENT: Earth
PLANET: Venus
ORIGIN: Mexico, Central America, and South America

(It's usually sold as a twig, as shown here.)

MEDICINAL PROPERTIES:
Purifying and relaxing.

MAGICAL PROPERTIES:
It's one of the most popular plants in the magical world. For some groups, it's a sacred tree, and using it in a spiritual way without the proper context or knowledge could be considered cultural appropriation.

It's used to smudge and cleanse negative energies from a space, from a work tool, or from ourselves. Remember to open the windows before using it. Light it with the flame of a candle or match and let yourself take in the scent. You'll notice its powerful effect in a matter of seconds. It's also common to use it in shavings, as an essential oil, or in the form of a stick.

FRANKINCENSE

(Boswellia spp.)

GENDER: Male
ELEMENT: Fire
PLANET: Sun
ORIGIN: Arabian Peninsula and Horn of Africa

MEDICINAL PROPERTIES:
Beneficial for asthma and other respiratory conditions.

MAGICAL PROPERTIES:
It accompanies the fulfillment of desires, and it attracts luck and good energies. It's used in rituals for abundance and fortune.

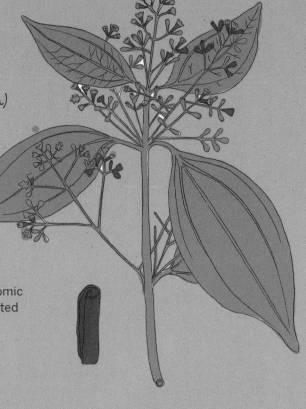

CINNAMON
(Cinnamomum verum)

GENDER: Female
ELEMENT: Earth
PLANET: Venus
ORIGIN: Sri Lanka

MEDICINAL PROPERTIES:
Antiseptic and aphrodisiac.

MAGICAL PROPERTIES:
It's often used in rituals for economic prosperity, but above all, it is related to love and sexual attraction.

SUGAR
(Saccharum officinarum)

GENDER: Male
ELEMENT: Earth
PLANET: Mercury
ORIGIN: New Guinea

MEDICINAL PROPERTIES:
Relieves discomfort and anxiety and helps with the digestion of proteins.

MAGICAL PROPERTIES:
It's often used in rituals of attraction and love. It's a good vegan substitute for honey, which is often used for similar purposes. It's usually used to dress candles for love spells and to sweeten difficult situations.

LILY
(Lilium spp.)

GENDER: Female
ELEMENT: Earth
PLANET: Venus
ORIGIN: Eurasia and North America

MEDICINAL PROPERTIES:
Diuretic and sedative.

MAGICAL PROPERTIES:
Often associated with peace, harmony, and well-being. It's said that a house with lilies is full of these qualities, or that lilies help attract them.

If you let the root of a lily dry in the sun for a month and then grind it with your mortar, it becomes a powder widely used in love rituals, especially in a romantic relationship.

It's a symbol of power, elegance, and purity. It's related to the French monarchy.

NETTLE
(Urtica spp.)

GENDER: Male
ELEMENT: Fire
PLANET: Sun
ORIGIN: Global

MEDICINAL PROPERTIES:
Soothes joint and muscle pain and allergies; a good source of antioxidants. (It's one of the most widely used plants in medicine; however, be careful when handling it, because it can cause a burning sensation if directly in contact with the skin.)

MAGICAL PROPERTIES:
Its main function is protective, driving away enemies and the evil desires of those who can harm us.

POISONOUS PLANTS

There are some toxic plants to be aware of, and some can even cause death. The following plants have been used at times throughout the history of magic to make poisons. Do not consume these in any way, shape, or form. In most cases, it's dangerous to even handle them. A great amount of knowledge of botany and magic is needed to understand how to handle these plants and safely incorporate them into practice. These plants have incredibly powerful energy.

BELLADONNA
(Atropa belladonna)

GENDER: Female
ELEMENT: Earth
PLANET: Venus
ORIGIN: Eurasia

MAGICAL PROPERTIES:
It's related to the goddesses Hecate and Persephone. Even in small doses, it is lethal. It's associated with witches, as it causes hallucinations.

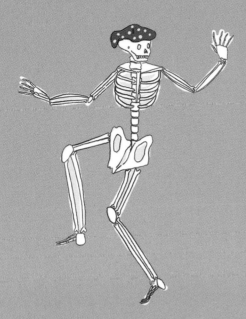

OLEANDER
(Nerium oleander)

Considered the most poisonous plant in the world. It has very showy fuchsia flowers and is usually found in gardens.

COMMON ACONITE
(Aconitum napellus)

It's a plant with blue or violet flowers that can be lethal.

CASTOR BEAN
(Ricinus communis)

It comes from Africa; ingesting it can cause death.

HEMLOCK
(Cicuta matulata)

Cicutoxin, the element that makes this plant toxic, is more concentrated in the root, from which one of the most notorious poisons is extracted. It produces a violent death.

JIMSONWEED
(Datura stramonium)

This American native causes delirium and hallucinations, as well as death. The seeds are the most toxic.

YEW
(Taxus baccata)

It is native to most of Europe and northern Africa. Although it has some medicinal uses within the pharmaceutical industry, it's considered toxic.

INFUSE MAGIC INTO YOUR MORNING TEA OR COFFEE

Enjoy your drink in a quiet place.

Place the crystals (see chapter 5) corresponding to your intention next to your tea or coffee.

Think about your intention for the day while stirring your tea or coffee. Say it out loud if you like.

Stir with the spoon clockwise to attract and counterclockwise to let go or destroy.

Check the properties of each ingredient (on the facing page).

INGREDIENTS FOR INFUSIONS

Coffee
Stimulant.

Sugar
Love, purification, attraction.

Honey/Syrup
Bonds, attraction, love.

Milk/Cream
Nurturing, protection, power.

Soy Milk
Work success, protection.

Coconut Milk
Protection, cleansing.

Oat Milk
Reinforcement, prosperity.

Almond Milk
Prosperity, wealth, wisdom.

Vanilla
Happiness, love, good luck.

Cinnamon
Protection, prosperity.

Mint Tea
Decongestion, clarity; soothes stomach pain.

Chamomile
Relaxation; helps with sleep.

Black Tea
Strength, energy; drives away negativity.

White Tea
Cleansing, protection.

Green Tea
Energy, immunity, cleansing.

Rooibos
Strength, energy, security.

Chai
Calm, protection, prosperity.

Matcha
Clarity, passion, love, energy.

Ginger
Balance, clarity.

Cocoa
Love, clarity.

SMUDGE STICKS

Although we've already covered the properties of herbs and what smudge sticks are, here is a summary of the most common herbal bundles that you can find in specialized stores. Remember, you can make them yourself by tying fresh herbs with natural fibers, chosen according to your intention. You can charge them under the light of the full moon to give them even more power.

Mugwort

Lavender

Juniper

White Sage

Dragon's Blood

Palo Santo

Rosemary

Cedar

Mugwort: Traditionally used to cleanse spaces of negative energy. It's also known to stimulate lucid dreaming; if you have this intention, burn this herb before going to sleep.

Lavender: Often used for cleansing, spiritual protection, and to enhance psychic gifts. It attracts positive energy and promotes tranquility, peace, and well-being.

Juniper: Often used to cleanse and energize. It brings strength to both mind and body when we need an extra boost of energy.

White Sage: It's the world's best-known spiritual and ritual cleansing plant. It's used to transform the energy in a room as well as for medicinal, purification, and cleansing purposes.

Dragon's Blood: This is a resin that is applied to bundles of white sage and gives them a reddish tinge. It's very potent and is often used in deep cleansings to ward off negative energies and unwanted entities.

Palo Santo: This sacred wood cleanses negative energy, purifies, and stimulates creativity and intuition. It's used in many rituals for several purposes; it helps to draw in a greater spiritual connection.

Rosemary: This is a very powerful cleansing and purifying herb, both for spaces and objects as well as for us. It's associated with the sun and masculine energy.

Cedar: It's traditionally used to cleanse negative energy when moving into a new house. A cedar twig should be burned as a cleansing ritual.

ESSENTIAL OILS

Essential oils have the same properties as the plants they are derived from. Below is a list of the most well-known essential oils and their associations. Adding a few drops of essential oil to your rituals enhances your intention. They are also common in spells, meditation, and aromatherapy.

Courage
Pepper
Parsley
Nettle
Chives
Radish

Fertility
Cinnamon
Mint
Cilantro
Sugar

Happiness
Cinnamon
Mint
Calendula
Aniseed

Well-being
Chamomile
Aniseed
Cinnamon
Angelica

Intuition
Lemongrass
Orange
Sage
Palo santo
Rosemary

Love
Cinnamon
Sugar
Cocoa
Vanilla
Lavender

Luck
Heather
Pepper
Spearmint
Sandalwood
Nutmeg

Money
Patchouli
Parsley
Ginger
Chamomile
Dill
Cinnamon

Peace
Marjoram
Sage
Palo santo
Lily

Protection
Angelica
Parsley
Nettle
Clove
Garlic
Mint

Success
Laurel
Chamomile
Rosemary
Saffron
Celery

Travel
Mustard
Parsley
Fennel
Marjoram

Wisdom
Laurel
Chamomile
Sage
Thyme

5.
THE POWER OF STONES

Using Stones for Magic

- Clean and charge a crystal.
- Rings according to intentions.
- Types of stones.
- Chakras.

CLEANING A CRYSTAL

Often, the concept of charging a crystal is confused with that of cleaning a crystal. They are two different things. Crystals absorb energy so it is necessary to clean each one to expel old, negative energy or energy that simply doesn't belong to us. You can clean your quartz, crystals, or stones as often as needed, but the most common time to do it is during a waning moon (page 190). The following illustrate different ways to clean any tool.

White Sage

Palo Santo

Visualization

Incense

Salt

Sunlight

Moonlight

Earth

Tibetan Singing Bowl

Meditation Music

Water with Salt

Florida Water

CHARGING CRYSTALS

Once cleansed, the crystals must be charged or activated. They can be charged with a natural element, such as sunlight or moonlight, but more often they are charged with our personal energy and programmed with a specific intention when we focus our energy on them.

The most common methods to charge crystals (or other tools) are the following (some are the same or similar to the methods used to clean a crystal, as seen opposite, but what matters is the intention you set):

- Run them through a stream of water (except for the crystals that should not get wet; see below).
- Put them in nature, in a garden or pot.
- Use sound vibrations, such as bells, cymbals, or singing.
- Place a clean quartz or amethyst on them.
- Simply hold the crystal in your hands.

CRYSTALS THAT SHOULD NOT GET WET

- Angelita
- Turquoise
- Kunzite
- Selenite
- Kyanite
- Malachite
- Calcite
- Labradorite
- Lapis lazuli

CRYSTALS THAT SHOULD NOT BE EXPOSED TO SUNLIGHT

- Aventurine
- Amethyst
- Aquamarine
- Beryl
- Citrine
- Kunzite
- Sapphire
- Fluorite
- Rose quartz
- Smoky quartz

THE SHAPES OF CRYSTALS

Aside from the fact that each stone has its own properties and uses, below is a list of crystals according to their shape, which qualifies, complements, or defines their ritual use.

Geode

This is a horizontal cut that's related to inner peace, tranquility, and calmness.

Uncut

Uncut minerals present their most natural form, so they have a spontaneous and strong energy.

Tip or generator

Tips or generators have an amplifying function, as they concentrate and direct energy. They're also used to charge energy.

Sphere

Spheres possess a soft energy that's related to the spiritual world and divination.

Pebble

The pebble has a smooth polish and natural shape, with a soft and calm energy.

Pyramid

The pyramid has a very powerful energy that is generally used to attract.

Double

Double-tipped minerals serve to absorb, transmute, and transform energy.

RINGS ACCORDING TO INTENTION

Willpower

Authority, Self-Esteem

Emotional Stability

Creativity

Sexuality, Magnetism

We can activate jewelry, especially rings, to attract the type of energy we want.

We can also choose not only on which finger to wear our ring, but also what type of stone to wear. Following are the most well-known crystals and their common uses.

TYPES OF CRYSTALS

WHITE QUARTZ

White quartz is one of the most popular and powerful stones. Its properties are purifying; it cleanses negative energies and gives peace and harmony to the wearer. It's a good companion in healing, concentration, and meditation. You can use it to replace any other hard-to-find stones in your rituals.

AURA QUARTZ

Aura or rainbow quartz is related to relaxation and peace of mind or spirit. It's not a natural quartz, since it's obtained through a chemical process; nevertheless, it's a crystal with very powerful properties associated with harmonizing communication and environments, and reducing stress. Since it's chemically modified, not everyone believes it maintains its properties, but I think it does.

LABRADORITE

Labradorite is one of my favorite stones. Its iridescent blue reflections on the surface of green and black tones make this stone hypnotic.

It's related to spirituality, intuition, and divination and helps to develop psychic abilities. It also brings forth self-confidence, imagination, and introspection.

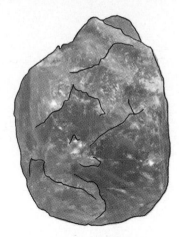

ROSE QUARTZ

Rose quartz is also one of the most popular stones, and its pink tones, in addition to transmitting peace and balance, associate it with the goddess Aphrodite. The properties of this stone are therefore related to love, beauty, and desire. It's said that if you wear a rose quartz, besides having greater self-esteem and feeling more confident, you will attract love.

AMETHYST

Amethyst is one of the basics needed to start your collection of magical stones. It's associated with the god Mercury. Therefore, it favors qualities related to the mind, balancing them. It enhances memory and concentration, and helps to steady our mind so that we suffer less emotional pain in adverse situations. It's a very energetically intense stone.

LAPIS LAZULI

In ancient Egypt, lapis lazuli was considered a magical stone; it was used to make numerous pieces of jewelry and amulets. It's a natural harmonizer of our inner selves: It helps balance our most disparate parts so that we can achieve harmony and stability, especially between our rational and emotional sides.

OPAL

Opal is related to psychic abilities: intuition, mediumship, and the connection with other planes of reality. It also stimulates creativity and imagination. It connects our mind and spirit to make the most of both working together.

OBSIDIAN

Like most black stones, obsidian is fundamentally related to protection. It's said to protect the user by absorbing the negative energies of the environment where it is found. Another of its most common uses is related to its transmutational power, cleansing and purifying us.

FLUORITE

Fluorite, with its various colors, has a delicate and subtle energy related to the spiritual world. It helps us in the development of virtues such as balance, order, cleansing, and purification and also in elevating our vibration.

GARNET

Garnet is related to our personal courage, power, and self-affirmation. It's a very useful stone when our energy is low or we feel insecure, as well as in periods of crisis.

AGATE

Agate is a versatile stone that can bring us protection, self-esteem, and security. Above all, it's used with the intention of achieving balance across our different planes: mental, physical, and spiritual.

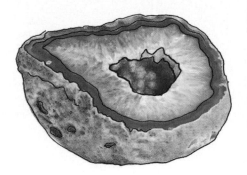

CORAL

Coral is related to the sun. It has a long history of attracting success, wealth, and abundance. It's even mentioned in the Bible. It helps us achieve our goals—especially with work or money—by giving us that necessary "push."

APATITE

This blue stone is ideal for shy or introverted people seeking to find greater self-confidence. It helps us achieve, above all, better speaking skills so we can communicate more effectively with others.

AVENTURINE

Aventurine is associated with prosperity, calmness, and balance; it has a powerful yet tranquil and gentle energy. It's related primarily to well-being and happiness.

JASPER

Red jasper brings strength, security, and self-confidence. It provides vitality to the body and mind, so it is a very useful stone while you're studying or performing any physical or intellectual effort.

AQUAMARINE

Aquamarine is related to emotions, empathy, gentleness, and intuition, which makes it kindred to water signs (Pisces, Cancer, Scorpio). It's useful if we want to encourage these qualities in ourselves or in others.

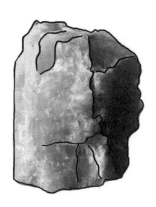

TIGER'S EYE

Tiger's eye is a powerful stone that is related to spiritual protection, promoting strength and self-confidence and making us feel more powerful.

ANGELITE

As its name indicates, this stone is related to angels and archangels. It helps keep us connected with them and, therefore, has a protective function.

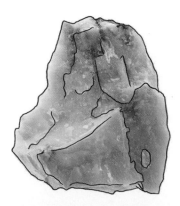

DALMATIAN STONE

This is a type of jasper whose distinctive appearance is reminiscent of a Dalmatian's coat. It facilitates the assimilation of change and the ability to adapt to new circumstances, whether adverse or simply different.

JADE

Jade has a dual function. On the one hand, it is considered a protective stone. On the other, it's considered a talisman to attract romance or true love into one's life.

MOONSTONE

The moonstone, as its name indicates, is associated with the moon and the goddess Selene. It is also related to witches, intuition, and psychic abilities.

SUNSTONE

As its name indicates, it's associated with the sun and, therefore, with the sun's associated virtues. Extroversion, personal charm, happiness, and enjoyment are qualities linked to this stone.

WITCHES STONE

This type of stone, found on beaches, has the defining feature of a hole formed by water. It brings protection and increases psychic abilities and vision.

AMBER

Amber is the fossilized resin of conifers. Its main use is for protection, and it favors stability and balance between our mind and spirit.

HEMATITE

Hematite is a protective stone. It also brings balance and stability to our core so that negative external energies cannot affect us.

SMOKY QUARTZ

Smoky quartz is characterized by bringing self-confidence and the necessary strength to achieve our purposes.

SELENITE

Selenite is one of the most popular stones and one of the basics in a collection of magical stones. It's used to harmonize and cleanse and to balance spaces and also our inner selves. It's usually bar shaped.

ONYX

Onyx is a protective stone that enhances self-confidence and empowers us with courage and initiative.

TOURMALINE

Tourmaline is one of the most important protective stones. It captures the negative energy of the environment and transmutes it. It helps in protection rituals and to eliminate blockages in limiting situations.

CITRINE

Citrine is one of the most important and powerful minerals in the spiritual world. It's related to positive energy, sunshine, clarity of ideas, happiness, and all that is good in life. It helps attract luck and abundance.

CHAKRAS

Chakras are energetic points in our body. If they are obstructed, energy does not flow properly, and energy blockages occur. To balance them, we can use a series of crystals related to each of the seven energy points.

Crown chakra

Associated with understanding and will.

Stones: white quartz, moonstone, amethyst, labradorite.

Third eye chakra

Associated with imagination and spiritual connection.

Stones: sodalite, lapis lazuli, sapphire, azulite.

Throat chakra

Associated with power.

Stones: turquoise, aquamarine, blue howlite, blue agate.

Heart chakra

Associated with love.

Stones: rose quartz, rhodonite, amazonite, green opal.

Solar plexus chakra

Associated with wisdom.

Stones: citrine, topaz, amber, tiger's eye.

Sacral chakra

Associated with order.

Stone: carnelian.

Root chakra

Associated with sex and life.

Stones: obsidian, tourmaline, coral.

6.
ANGELS, ARCHANGELS, SPIRIT GUIDES, AND GODDESSES

These are all beings of the spiritual plane. Though it's not necessary to work with them, it is good to know what they are. Magic is not a religion, but we can draw on elements of some beliefs to develop our spiritual practice, as long as they resonate with us. This is just a short introduction to a very complex subject.

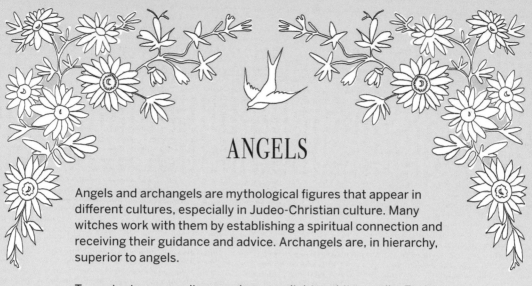

ANGELS

Angels and archangels are mythological figures that appear in different cultures, especially in Judeo-Christian culture. Many witches work with them by establishing a spiritual connection and receiving their guidance and advice. Archangels are, in hierarchy, superior to angels.

To contact our guardian angel, we can light a white candle. Each archangel corresponds to a color and day of the week, so we can light the appropriate candle to contact them.

"Angel numbers" are numbers that, when we see them repeatedly, may carry a message for us from our guardian angels. These numbers can also be linked to our spirit guides (page 81).

111
Trust your intuition. New beginnings.

222
You are at the right place at the right time.

333
You are being protected and guided.

444
Let yourself flow.

555
Something new is on the way.

666
It is time to grow and improve.

777
Good luck.

888
Everything is positioning itself where it should be.

999
Let go.

ARCHANGELS

There are seven archangels, and each has its own associations.

RAPHAEL
Green
Thursday

MICHAEL
Blue
Sunday

JOPHIEL
Yellow
Monday

GABRIEL
Light blue
Wednesday

URIEL
Orange
Friday

CHAMUEL
Pink
Tuesday

ZADKIEL
Purple
Saturday

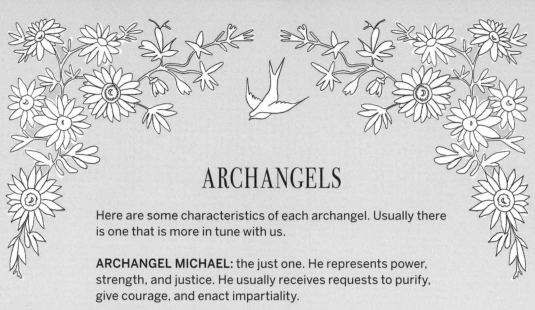

ARCHANGELS

Here are some characteristics of each archangel. Usually there is one that is more in tune with us.

ARCHANGEL MICHAEL: the just one. He represents power, strength, and justice. He usually receives requests to purify, give courage, and enact impartiality.

ARCHANGEL JOPHIEL: the illuminator. He's associated with intelligence, mental clarity, and wisdom. When we must make a crucial decision, we usually turn to him.

ARCHANGEL CHAMUEL: the lover. He's associated with relationships (whether you have a partner or not), with bonds, and with love. He can also protect us against envy and evil desires.

ARCHANGEL GABRIEL: the messenger. He's associated with clear, calm, and accurate communication. Also with art, inspiration, and the search for tranquility.

ARCHANGEL RAPHAEL: the healer. He's related to health, and not only physical health but also mental and spiritual health. He will help us overcome difficult moments related to our mood.

ARCHANGEL URIEL: the strong one. This archangel is associated with self-esteem, self-worth, and self-image. Also, with material resources and work life.

ARCHANGEL ZADKIEL: the forgiving one. He oversees the transformation of our feelings of regret into forgiveness, acceptance, and love. He can help us overcome selfish attitudes.

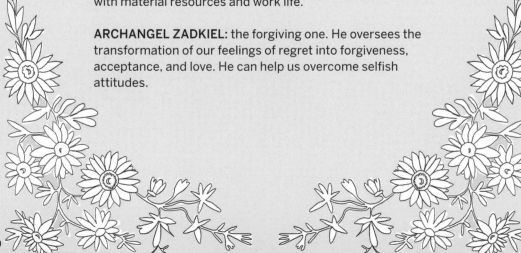

SPIRIT GUIDES

Spirit guides are nonmaterial beings who protect us from the immaterial plane of reality. We can connect with them through meditation, introspection, and self-knowledge, and we should be attentive to the messages they send us, for example through colors or numbers. Keeping a dream diary can be useful in helping us track and interpret their signs. One of the most common signs they send are bird feathers in the following colors:

GRAY
Peace will
soon come.

RED
Your spiritual
journey is
beginning.

PURPLE
Communicate
your feelings.

BLUE
Your psychic abilities
are revealing themselves.

PINK
Love and children
are on the way.

WHITE
Change is coming.

YELLOW
You're on the
right track.

BLACK
Your guide is
protecting you.

GREEN
You or someone
you love is healing.

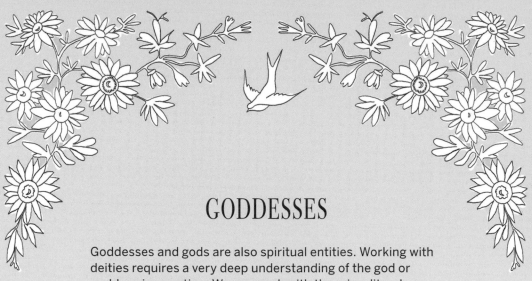

GODDESSES

Goddesses and gods are also spiritual entities. Working with deities requires a very deep understanding of the god or goddess in question. We can work with them in a literal way (assuming that gods are spiritual entities belonging to specific cultures and being respectful of them), or we can be inspired by qualities of each deity for our personal and spiritual development.

The topic of goddesses is thrilling, but it's also incredibly extensive, and explaining how to work with the deities of the main pantheons could be the subject of another book entirely.

However, La Meiga Dorada, one of my favorite witches, taught me that for every deity, or even ordinary person, there is an egregore. An egregore is the energy popular leaders, goddesses, or deities transmit. The more people follow or ask for the egregore, the more powerful it becomes, because there are thousands or even millions of people moving energy in its name.

Witches usually work with female deities; those of the Greek pantheon are among the most popular, such as Hecate (goddess of magic) or Aphrodite (goddess of love, beauty, and desire).

7.
THE WHEEL OF ANNUAL PAGAN FESTIVITIES

On every solstice, equinox, and point in between, we celebrate nature and ourselves. Each holiday marks a perfect time to get together with friends, cook with seasonal ingredients, and decorate our magical space to better connect with nature and with our inner selves. These festivities are related to Celtic culture as well as to contemporary events and those in other cultures.

BELTANE

MAY 1

Beltane is the first holiday of the magical year (both the magical and astrological years begin in April with Aries season). It celebrates fertility, life, and the proximity of summer. Below is a way you can celebrate a Beltane party with your friends.

MAYPOLE

The maypole is a traditional Celtic game typically played during this season. In Spain it's celebrated in the north (especially in Galicia and Cantabria). It consists of weaving colored ribbons around a wooden pole.

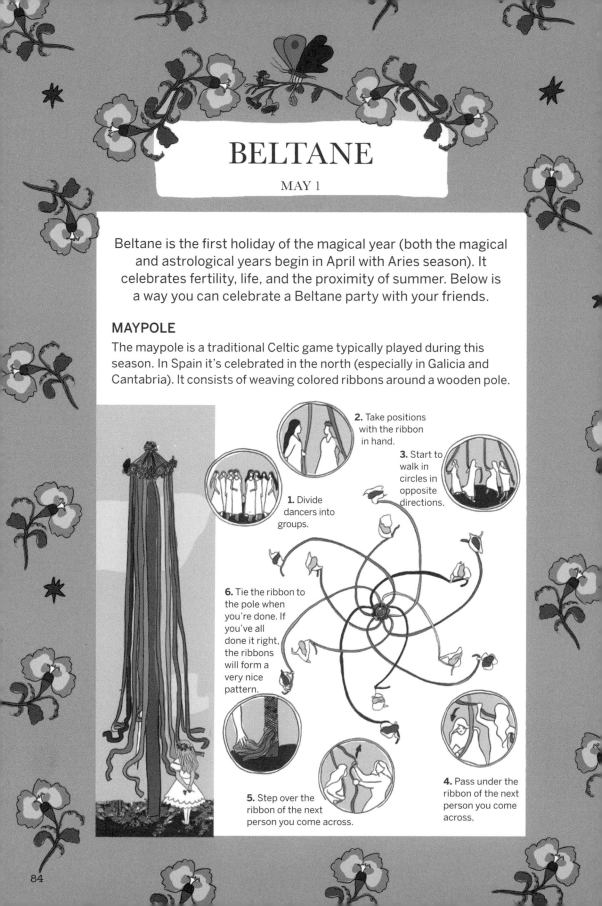

2. Take positions with the ribbon in hand.

3. Start to walk in circles in opposite directions.

1. Divide dancers into groups.

6. Tie the ribbon to the pole when you're done. If you've all done it right, the ribbons will form a very nice pattern.

5. Step over the ribbon of the next person you come across.

4. Pass under the ribbon of the next person you come across.

BELTANE TRADITIONS

Here are some festive elements to inspire and guide you in how to decorate your altar or party.

FLOWERS
Daisy
Dandelion
Lilac
Daffodil
Rose

HERBS
Mint
Spearmint
Mugwort
Woodruff

TREES
Oak
Pine
Willow
Birch

STONES
Aventurine
Emerald
Jade
Malachite
Rhodonite
Rose quartz

KEY WORDS
Abundance
Fertility
Ancestry
Growth
Love
Union

COLORS
Green
Blush pink
White
Yellow
Lilac

SYMBOLS AND ELEMENTS
Bonfire
Offerings
Bells
Flowers
Maypole
Singing and dancing
Planting trees
Gardening
Honey
Cake
Lemonade
Punch

TAROT
The Empress
The High Priestess
The Magician

ANIMALS
Bee
Cow
Rabbit
Sheep
Bird

MAGICAL INTENTION
Fertility
Manifestation
New ideas
Purification
Union
Spells

DRESS CODE

Ideally, wear white and decorate your clothes and hair with seasonal flowers.

FLOWER CROWN

Follow these illustrations to make a crown.

BELTANE PARTY RECIPES

Here are some traditional recipes for this holiday. Prepare them with your guests or serve them when they arrive. Ideally, have a picnic or celebrate in a garden.

BELTANE LEMONADE

Lemons: longevity, purification, friendship.

Spearmint: healing, love, psychic powers.

Ginger: money, success, power.

Rosemary: protection, healing, cleansing.

Sugar: love, harmony, sweetness.

In a glass jar or serving pitcher, mix cold water with fresh lemon juice, spearmint leaves, grated ginger, and rosemary sprigs. Sweeten with sugar to taste. Chill, add slices of lemon for decoration, and serve.

BELTANE COOKIES

SERVES 12

½ cup butter, plus a dab for greasing the baking sheet

2 cups flour, sifted

½ cup sugar

1 egg

1 teaspoon rose essence (edible)

Edible rose petals, for decoration

Preheat the oven to 375°F.

In a large bowl, mix the butter and sifted flour.

Add the sugar, egg, and rose essence and continue mixing with your hands. The dough should be a compact mixture. If it sticks to your fingers, add a little flour.

Roll out the dough with a rolling pin to form a sheet about ½ inch thick.

Use a 3-inch cookie cutter to form the cookies.

Grease a baking pan with a little butter and place the cookies on the pan.

Decorate them with rose petals.

Bake for 8 to 10 minutes.

BELTANE SPELL

To end the party, perform this spell with your guests or alone at your altar.

YOU WILL NEED

- 1 white candle, or Beltane candle, per person
- 1 piece of paper, per person
- A fire or bonfire to burn herbs and flowers, preferably from the list on page 85, outside
- Pink ink or pink pencil

METHOD

Each person writes down on paper things they'd like to achieve in life, and then throws the papers into the fire of Beltane. We hold hands, forming a circle around the fire, and focus our energy on their fulfillment.

BELTANE CANDLES

Dress the candles (page 31) with the following elements:

- Rose petals
- Lavender
- Mint
- Honey (or sugar)

BELTANE RITUAL BATH

Give your guests a bottle of these salts as a gift at the end of the party, or make them for yourself if you are celebrating alone.

Mix the following ingredients in your mortar and pestle by the light of the full moon.

YOU WILL NEED

- Rose petals
- Lavender
- Mint
- Sugar
- Ritualized coarse salt
- 3 drops of rose hip oil
- 1 capful of Florida water

METHOD

Add all ingredients to the bathwater and take a bath. Without rinsing yourself, get out of the bathtub and pat dry. This bath serves to attract love and abundance, to help you feel more self-confident, and to cleanse negative energy.

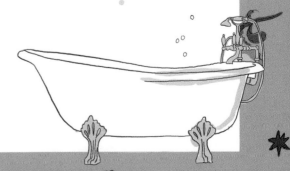

LITHA

SUMMER SOLSTICE

Litha is one of the most important holidays, celebrated on the day with the most hours of sunshine and the shortest night of the year, and it's related specifically to light, life, and the sun. It's a night full of energetic intensity. In some places a bonfire is skipped; in others celebrants make queimada (page 92) and perform other types of rituals. Below are my suggestions for how to celebrate Litha, but there are many other ways.

LITHA WATER OR ST. JOHN WATER

In Galicia, El Bierzo, and other areas of Celtic influence, there is a tradition of making water with sacred plants on the day of the solstice. We put the water in a basin with the seven herbs of St. John on the night of St. John's Day or on the night of the summer solstice itself. We leave the basin outside to rest under the moonlight. The next morning, we wash our face with this water to attract abundance and happiness.

YOU WILL NEED

Water: In some traditions it must come from seven different sources. But bottled or tap water can be used instead. I collect the water from a spring near my house.

Herbs from the eve of St. John: You can use these seven herbs or simply use what's available in your area. The tradition is to collect them, but it's okay to buy them from an herb shop too.

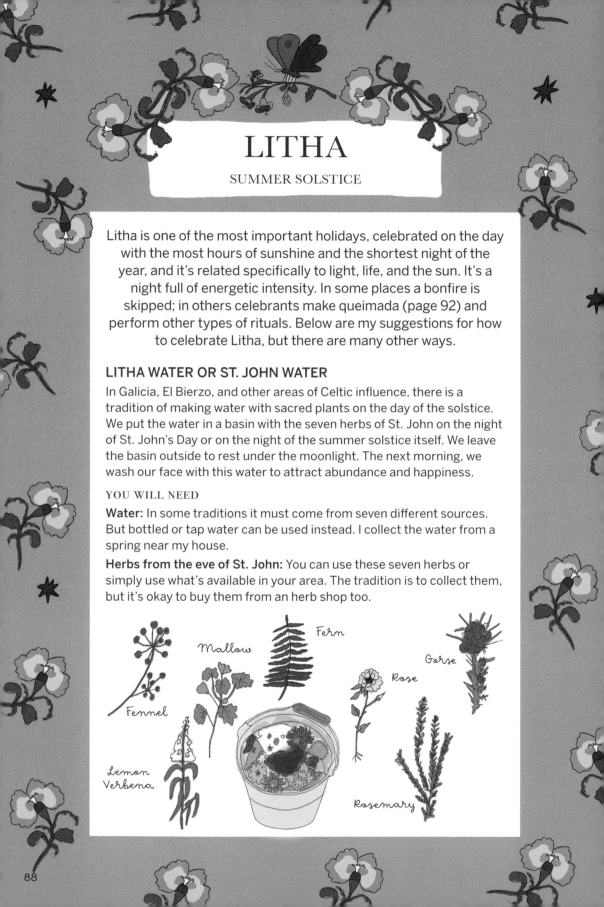

Fennel

Mallow

Fern

Rose

Gorse

Lemon Verbena

Rosemary

LITHA TRADITIONS

Here are some festive elements to inspire and guide you in how to decorate your altar or party.

HERBS
Fern
St. John's wort
Thyme
Sage

TREES
Fig
Peach
Plum

STONES
Diamond
Citrine
Tiger's eye
Amber

KEY WORDS
Abundance
Fertility
Renovation
Life
Fire
Power
Beauty

COLORS
Yellow
Gold
White
Orange

SYMBOLS AND ELEMENTS
Bonfire
Light
Sun
White candles
Yellow candles
Gathering herbs
Helios
Hydromel
Queimada

TAROT
The Sun
The Fool
The Queen of Pentacles

ANIMALS
Bull
Horse
Sparrow
Eagle
Butterfly

MAGICAL INTENTION
Vigor
Fertility

SUNFLOWERS

Sunflowers represent the sun. They can be used to decorate your magical space or your party.

DRESS CODE

Ideally, wear white and warm tones such as yellow, gold jewelry, and yellow flowers that are associated with the sun.

The queimada is my favorite Litha ritual, customary in Galicia and El Bierzo, and usually performed on the summer solstice and on special occasions.

LITHA PARTY RECIPES

Here are some traditional recipes for this holiday. Prepare them with your guests or serve them when they arrive. Ideally, have a picnic or celebrate in a garden.

LITHA TEA

Black tea, brewed and cooled

Fresh mint

Sugar

Raspberries

In a glass jar or serving pitcher, mix the brewed black tea and mint leaves. Sweeten with sugar to taste. Mix in fresh raspberries before serving.

LITHA VEGETABLE COCA

SERVES 12

Spring onions

1 bunch of chard

1 red bell pepper

1 tomato

Garlic

Puff pastry

Olive oil

Paprika

Salt

Preheat the oven to 350°F.

Clean the vegetables and cut them all into strips. Leave the garlic cloves whole, or finely chop them if you prefer a less intense flavor.

Place the puff pastry sheet on a 9 by 13-inch baking pan.

Prick the pastry all over with a fork so that it does not puff up, drizzle olive oil over it, and top with the vegetables and spices to your liking.

Bake for about 30 minutes, until golden.

Tip: To crisp the dough, bake it for about 5 minutes before adding the vegetables.

LITHA SPELL:
MAKE A WISH ON A FAIRY

To end the party, perform this spell with your guests or alone at your altar.

YOU WILL NEED

- 1 white candle
- 1 small wooden box
- 3 bay leaves and 3 dandelions
- Paper
- Pencil

METHOD

Write a letter to the fairies with a wish; it's important that the wish is of pure intention. Put all the elements in the box (you can add elements that are related to your wish, such as quartz or other plants) and ask the fairies to make your wish come true. Keep the box until the wish is fulfilled. (Fairy time is different from ours, so it may take a long time for your wish to come true.)

LITHA CANDLES

The beeswax candle from chapter 3 is perfect for this holiday, as it's related to the sun and abundance. Although you can also dress the candles with some of the plants from the list on page 89.

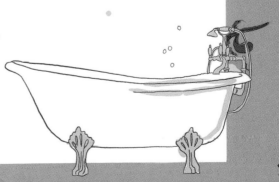

LITHA RITUAL BATH

Give your guests a bottle of these salts as a gift at the end of the party, or make them for yourself if you are celebrating alone.

Mix the following ingredients in your mortar and pestle by the light of the full moon.

YOU WILL NEED

- Sugar
- 3 drops of lemon essential oil
- 3 drops of orange essential oil
- Dried citrus slices
- Coarse sea salt
- 1 small glass of solar water

METHOD

Add all ingredients to the bathwater and take a bath. Without rinsing yourself, get out of the bathtub and pat dry. This bath serves to boost the sun's energy, charge us with it, and make us feel revitalized, in addition to cleansing our energy.

QUEIMADA

In El Bierzo and Galicia, one of the most popular traditions to take part in on the night of the solstice is a queimada. It's the reading of an incantation (opposite) while making an alcoholic drink with sugar, lemon, and coffee, which is later shared. A special earthenware container is usually used, accompanied by cups and an earthenware ladle, which is used only for this ritual. While one person makes the queimada, another recites the incantation.

Orujo
½ cup sugar, plus a pinch for starting the fire
Rind of ½ lemon
7 coffee beans

Pour most of the orujo into an earthenware pot. Add the sugar, lemon rind, and coffee beans.

Add a bit of the remaining orujo and a pinch of sugar to your ladle. Set it on fire, then lower it slowly to the pot until the fire passes from the ladle to the pot.

Stir with the ladle, continuously bringing the sugar from the bottom of the pot up to the flames on the surface so that it caramelizes and the orujo begins to change color.

Continue in this way until the flames acquire a bluish color. You can now either remove the queimada from the heat and cover the pot to put out the flame or keep going until all the alcohol has burned off, leaving only sweet water with some coffee and lemon flavor. Authentic queimada is achieved if you remove it earlier; ideally it should burn for about 15 minutes.

CONXURO
(SPELL)

Owls, barn owls, toads, and witches;
goblins, demons, and devils;
spirits from the foggy fields, ravens,
salamanders, and witches;
erected tail of black cat
and all the spells of the healers . . .
Rotten stalks with holes,
home of worms and vermin,
fire of the Holy Company, hex, black spells,
the smell of the dead, thunder and lightning;
snout of the satyr and foot of the rabbit;
barking of a fox, little tail of marten,
howling of a dog, crier of death . . .
Sinful tongue of the evil woman
married to an old man;
Hell of Satan and Beelzebub,
fire of burning corpses,
conceited fires of the night of San Silvestre,
mutilated bodies of the indecent,
and farts from infernal asses . . .
Roar of the raging sea, omen of shipwrecks,
the useless womb of the unmarried woman,
the meow of cats in heat,
dirty fur of the badly calved goat,
and buck's twisted horns . . .
With this ladle I will raise the flames of this
fire which resembles that of
hell, and the witches will be
purified of all their mischievousness.
Some of them will run away riding their
broomsticks, going to bathe
in the sea of Fisterra.
Listen, listen! The roars that they make!
They are the witches being
purified in these spirited flames . . .
And when this brew goes down our throats,
we all will also be free
from evils of our soul
and from all enchantment.
Forces of Air, Land, Sea, and Fire!
I make this request to you:
If it is true that you have more power than human people,
remove evil from the earth here and now,
make the spirits of absent friends
participate with us in this queimada.

LAMMAS

LAMMAS (OR LUGHNASADH)

This holiday celebrates the ripening of the harvest, especially of cherries. It comes from the pagan custom of thanking the gods for the harvests obtained. These fruits serve as preparation for the autumn.

DECORATE YOUR ALTAR

WHEAT STRAW DOLLS

Making dolls with straw is common to many cultures. They are also called grain goddesses or harvest queens.

YOU WILL NEED

- 30 stems or straws of the wheat plant
- Hemp or cotton thread
- Scissors

METHOD

1. Tie head
2. Spread arms
3. Braid arms
4. Tie waist
5. Dress (optional)

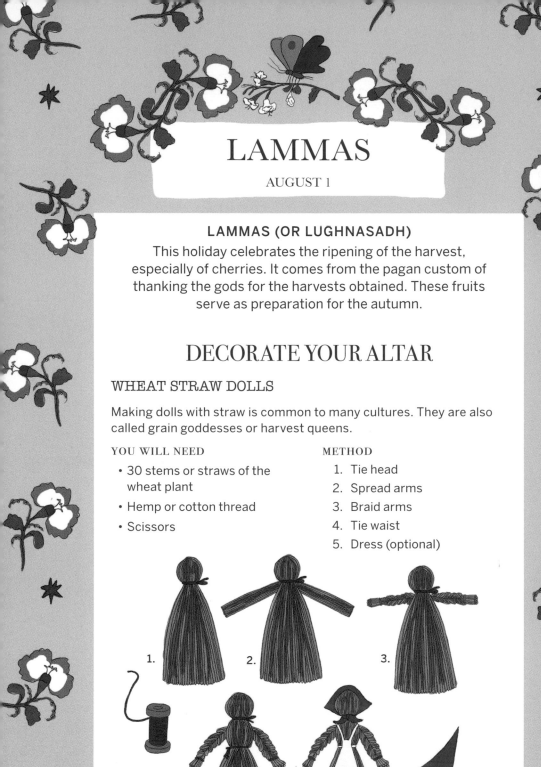

1.

2.

3.

4.

5.

94

LAMMAS TRADITIONS

Here are some festive elements to inspire and guide you in how to decorate your altar or party.

FLOWERS
Poppy
Peony
Rose

HERBS
Sandalwood
Verbena
Rosemary
Wheat
Corn

TREES
Oak
Pine
Willow
Birch

STONES
Citrine
Golden topaz
Moss agate
Obsidian
Yellow aventurine
Carnelian
Onyx

KEY WORDS
Harvest
Work
Rest

COLORS
Light brown
Beige
Ecru
Bronze
Orange

SYMBOLS AND ELEMENTS
Wheat
Corn
Cornucopia
Bread
Grain
Earth
Wheel
Chariot

DEITIES
Artemis
Ceres
Hathor

TAROT
The Chariot
The Wheel of Fortune

ANIMALS
Crow
Pig
Rooster

MAGICAL INTENTION
Gratitude
Abundance
Economy
Growth
Transformation
Strength
Protection
Ancestors

DRESS CODE

Ideally, wear colorful clothes, using cotton, wool, or other natural fibers (depending on your region). Braid your hair, or make a crown from the stems or straws of the wheat plant to decorate your hair, an activity that you can do at the Lammas party itself.

LAMMAS PARTY RECIPES

Here are some traditional recipes for this holiday. Prepare them with your guests or serve them when they arrive. Ideally, have a picnic or celebrate in a garden.

LAMMAS COCKTAIL

1 (25-ounce) bottle of cider

1 cinnamon stick

½ apple, sliced

½ cup red wine

Pour the cider into a jar and add the cinnamon and apple. Allow it to macerate for 10 days.

Once the time has elapsed, filter the mixture, pour it into a bottle, and add the red wine. Serve warm, hot, or cold, to taste.

LAMMAS BREAD

1⅓ cups warm water

½ ounce baker's yeast

2½ teaspoons sugar

2½ tablespoons extra-virgin olive oil, plus more for greasing

3 cups flour, plus more for sprinkling

1¾ teaspoons salt

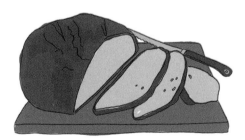

Preheat the oven to 390°F.

Pour the water into a large bowl, add the yeast and sugar, and stir.

Add the oil and half of the flour, stir until there are no lumps, and let stand for 20 minutes, covering the bowl with a cloth.

Add the rest of the flour, and the salt, and mix until a thick dough is formed.

Sprinkle a surface with flour, grease your hands with oil, and knead the dough into a flattened ball. Make two intersecting cuts with a knife.

Place the bread on a greased baking sheet.

Bake for 45 minutes, until golden. The loaf should sound hollow when tapped.

LAMMAS SPELL

For the festivity, make a spell powder charged with this holiday's energy. Use the powder all year long for intentions corresponding to the festivity.

YOU WILL NEED

- Mortar and pestle
- 3 tablespoons verbena
- 3 tablespoons rose petals
- 3 tablespoons marigold petals
- 1 tablespoon sandalwood powder

METHOD

Grind all the ingredients in the mortar and pestle and leave it on your altar for Lammas. (You can also charge the powder with moonlight.) Store the mixture in glass jars for use throughout the year.

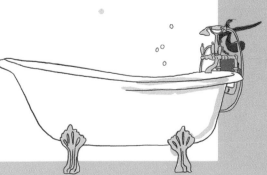

LAMMAS CANDLES

Dress the candles (page 31) with the following elements:

- Verbena
- Marigold
- Rose
- Ground wheat grains

LAMMAS RITUAL BATH

You can give your guests a bottle of these salts as a gift at the end of the party, or you can make them for yourself if you are celebrating alone.

Mix the following ingredients in your mortar and pestle by the light of the full moon.

YOU WILL NEED

- Rose petals
- Marigold
- Verbena
- 1 teaspoon cornstarch
- Ritualized coarse salt
- 1 drop of rosemary oil

METHOD

Add all ingredients to the bathwater and take a bath. Without rinsing yourself, get out of the bathtub and pat dry. This bath serves to thank ourselves for our inner strength and to ask ourselves to continue growing and becoming stronger.

MABON

AUTUMNAL EQUINOX

This is the second harvest festival, which coincides with the autumn equinox. During this festivity, apples are sacred. Apples are associated with magic, witchcraft, and Persephone.

DECORATE YOUR ALTAR

AUTUMN WREATH

YOU WILL NEED

- Cotton thread or string
- Twigs
- Dried leaves
- Pinecones, apples, and nuts
- Metal ring

METHOD

Use the thread to weave the various elements around the ring, first the larger ones and then the rest, filling in the gaps.

WITCH'S BROOM

YOU WILL NEED

- Twigs
- Twine
- A stick

METHOD

Go for a walk in the garden and ask nature for permission to collect the different elements.

Use the twine to tie the twigs around the stick. Use the broom to clean your altar whenever you need it.

You can also use the broom as a protective amulet for your magical space.

MABON TRADITIONS

Here are some festive elements to inspire and guide you in how to decorate your altar or your party.

FLOWERS
Chrysanthemum
Calendula

HERBS
Sage
Myrtle
Basil
Nutmeg

STONES
Sapphire
Lapis lazuli
Amber
Tiger's eye
Smoky quartz
Hematite
Aventurine

KEY WORDS
Harvest
Autumn
Equinox
Baskets

COLORS
Brown
Ocher
Yellow
Orange
Red

**SYMBOLS
AND ELEMENTS**
Apples
Bread
Dry leaves
Branches
Mushrooms
Cornucopia
Apple pie
Pinecones
Nuts

DEITIES
Thor
Morgan
Persephone
Demeter

TAROT
The Empress
The Hanged Man
The World

ANIMALS
Blackbird
Owl
Squirrel
Wolf

**MAGICAL
INTENTION**
Change
Gratitude
Preparation
Wisdom
Wealth
Study

DRESS CODE

Ideally, wear brown and other autumnal colors, and make brooches or decorations with nuts or dried leaves. Incorporate leather and wool details to clothing and/or shoes.

MABON PARTY RECIPES

Here are some traditional recipes for this holiday. Prepare them with your guests or serve them when they arrive. Ideally, have a picnic or celebrate in a garden.

MABON TEA

SERVES 1

1 tablespoon rooibos

3 slices candied orange

1 cinnamon stick

2 star anise

In a glass jar or serving pitcher, infuse the tea, orange, cinnamon, and star anise in almost boiling water for 4 minutes, filter, and drink hot.

MABON BAKED APPLES

Butter

Apples

Honey

Walnuts

Dried apricots

Cinnamon

Star anise

Preheat the oven to 355°F. Grease a baking sheet with a little butter.

Remove the stem and core from the apples, leaving plenty of flesh around the holes in the middle.

Place the rest of the ingredients inside the apples' centers, reserving a few pieces of each ingredient to set around the apples on the sheet for decoration.

Bake for about 40 minutes; the time will depend on the type of apple. Watch until the flesh of the fruit becomes soft and begins to release sugar.

Eat warm. The baked apples can be served with vanilla ice cream, with whipped cream, or alone.

MABON SPELL

For this spell, you'll fill a jar with seasonal ingredients to help attract financial prosperity.

YOU WILL NEED

- 1 small glass jar
- 3 tablespoons sage
- 3 tablespoons basil
- 1 teaspoon cinnamon powder
- 1 teaspoon palo santo shavings
- Green wax (from 1 small candle)

METHOD

Think of the abundance you are attracting as you hold the jar in your hand and pour in the ingredients (see chapter 10 for more on spells in jars), then seal it with green wax.

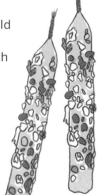

MABON CANDLES

Dress the candles (page 31) with the following elements:

- Palo santo shavings
- Small pieces of dried apple
- Sage
- Cinnamon

MABON RITUAL BATH

Give your guests a bottle of these salts as a gift at the end of the party, or you can make them for yourself if you are celebrating alone.

Mix the following ingredients in your mortar and pestle by the light of the full moon.

YOU WILL NEED

- Sage
- 1 drop of basil essential oil
- 3 drops of olive oil
- Coarse salt
- 1 capful of Florida water

METHOD

Add all ingredients to the bathwater and take a bath. Without rinsing yourself, get out of the bathtub and pat dry. This bath serves to work on abundance and economic prosperity.

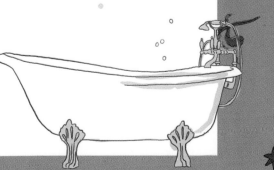

SAMHAIN

OCTOBER 31

The feast of Samhain marks the origin of Halloween, the night of the witches, and the day when the veil between the world of the living and the world of the dead is thinnest. It's a time to honor the dead and is one of the sabbats with the most powerful energy. In pop culture, it's associated with witches.

DECORATE YOUR ALTAR

SAMHAIN PUMPKIN

YOU WILL NEED

- 1 pumpkin
- 1 knife
- 1 pencil
- 1 tealight candle

METHOD

Cut out the top of the pumpkin in a circle around the stem. Once the lid has been removed, hollow out the inside of the pumpkin, so that it can be used as a lantern on the night of the thirty-first. Finally, trace the eyes, nose, and mouth with a pencil, and cut out holes so that the candlelight shines through.

SAMHAIN TRADITIONS

Here are some festive elements to inspire and guide you in how to decorate your altar or your party.

FLOWERS
Chrysanthemum

HERBS
Patchouli
Copal
Sandalwood
Palo santo

STONES
White quartz
Tourmaline
Onyx
Pyrite
Opal
Ruby
Diamond
Smoky quartz

KEY WORDS
Death
Witches
Rebirth

COLORS
Black
Orange
Gray
White

SYMBOLS AND ELEMENTS
Pumpkin
Death
Black cat
Cauldron
Skull
Night

DEITIES
Hecate
Freya
Lilith
Persephone

TAROT
Death
The Hermit

ANIMALS
Cat
Bat
Spider

MAGICAL INTENTION
Sacrifice
Shadows
Decisions
Divination
Mediumship
Cleansing

DRESS CODE

Ideally, wear dark colors. It's also a great time to dress up as a witch, vampire, ghost, and so forth, as is the Halloween tradition. On this holiday, children in some cultures go trick-or-treating. The day after Halloween is the holiday for other cultures. In Mexico, it's celebrated as the Day of the Dead, honoring deceased family members. In Spain and other places, it's celebrated as All Saints' Day.

SAMHAIN PARTY RECIPES

Here are some traditional recipes for this holiday. Prepare them with your guests or serve them when they arrive. Ideally, have a picnic or celebrate in a garden.

VEGAN VERSION OF LAMBSWOOL
(traditional Samhain drink)

4 cups oat milk

1 baked apple, peeled and diced

Brown sugar, to taste

1 dried vanilla bean

1 cinnamon stick

Orange peel

3 cloves

In a small pot, warm the oat milk with the apple, brown sugar, vanilla, cinnamon stick, orange peel, and cloves. Let the flavors infuse.

SPICED PUMPKIN SOUP

SERVES 4

1 small pumpkin, diced

1 onion, chopped

2 small potatoes, peeled and diced

1 tablespoon extra-virgin olive oil

Vegetable broth

Spices (cinnamon, pepper, and nutmeg)

Pumpkin seeds, for garnish

In a saucepan, sauté the pumpkin, onion, and potatoes in the olive oil for 5 minutes.

When the mixture is soft, add enough broth to cover the vegetables and cook for about 1 hour over low heat.

Add the cinnamon, pepper, and nutmeg to taste.

Garnish with pumpkin seeds.

SAMHAIN SPELL

ALTAR IN HONOR OF YOUR DECEASED LOVED ONES
This practice is inspired by the rituals of the Mexican Day of the Dead holiday and honors our ancestors. Place photos of your deceased relatives in your magical space, along with some items that they would like (food, objects, and so on). Write them a letter and light a white candle in their memory.

DIVINATION
On this special night, you can also practice divination and tarot. See chapter 9 for more on this.

SAMHAIN CANDLES

Use white or black candles and dress them (page 31) with the following elements:

- Palo santo chips
- Black salt (page 182)
- Dried patchouli
- Cloves

SAMHAIN RITUAL BATH

Give your guests a bottle of these salts as a gift at the end of the party, or you can make them for yourself if you are celebrating alone.

Mix the following ingredients in your mortar and pestle by the light of the full moon.

YOU WILL NEED

- 1 clove
- 1 drop of patchouli essential oil
- Coarse salt
- 1 capful of Florida water

METHOD
Add all ingredients to the bathwater and take a bath. Without rinsing yourself, get out of the bathtub and pat dry. This bath serves as an energy cleanse and works on your spiritual side.

YULE

WINTER SOLSTICE

Yule is the festival commemorating the winter solstice and is celebrated on the longest night of the year. On this holiday, ancient pagans ask for brighter days and welcome the return of the sun. It's a night of recollection and gratitude, where candles are lit in honor of the sun. Many of today's Christmas traditions, such as the Advent wreath, come from Yule.

DECORATE YOUR ALTAR

YULE TRUNK

YOU WILL NEED

1. A log
2. Rose hips
3. Mistletoe
4. Holly
5. 3 candles
6. Spruce leaves

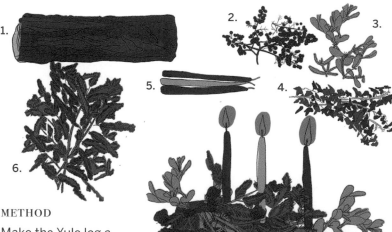

METHOD

Make the Yule log a month before Christmas. On the 12 days prior to the holiday, burn the candles. On the night of the solstice, the log is burned in the fireplace.

YULE TRADITIONS

Here are some festive elements to inspire and guide you in how to decorate your altar or party.

FLOWERS
Poinsettia
Lily

HERBS
Cardamom
Cinnamon
Clove
Saffron
Ivy

STONES
Moss agate
Amethyst
Onyx
Tanzanite
Turquoise

KEY WORDS
Empathy
Birth
Silence

COLORS
Dark green
Brown
Red
Gold
Silver

SYMBOLS AND ELEMENTS
Candelabra
Pines
Trunks
Ornaments
Mistletoe
Biscuits
Citrus
Tea
Sweets
Bells
Sleigh bells

DEITIES
Demeter
Brigid
Odin

TAROT
The Magician
The World
The Pentacles

ANIMALS
Reindeer
Bear
Horse

MAGICAL INTENTION
Wisdom
Cycles
Challenge
Family
Celebration
Study
Reflection

DRESS CODE

Ideally, wear your best clothes. Beige, white, red, and green hues are traditional for this party, but if we all were to dress in these colors for the occasion, it might look like we're in Whoville (home of the Grinch), so looking elegant is enough!

YULE PARTY RECIPES

Here are some traditional recipes for this holiday. Prepare them with your guests or serve them when they arrive. If weather permits, have a picnic or celebrate in a garden.

SPICED CHOCOLATE

Oat milk

Cardamom

Cinnamon

Clove

Whipped cream

Cocoa powder

In a small pot, warm the oat milk over low heat and add the spices to taste.
Serve warm, garnished with whipped cream and cocoa.

YULE LOG

FOR THE FILLING:

½ cup heavy cream

1 bar dark chocolate

FOR THE SPONGE CAKE:

4 eggs

½ cup sugar

½ cup + 2 tablespoons flour, sifted

1 pinch salt

½ teaspoon vanilla extract

Preheat the oven to 350°F.

In a small pot, warm the heavy cream over high heat until it boils. Add the chocolate and cook over low heat until it melts. Set aside.

In a bowl, beat the eggs with the sugar until stiff peaks form.

Gently fold the sifted flour and salt into the eggs. Mix in the vanilla.

Spread the egg mixture on a greased 13 by 18-inch baking sheet and bake for 10 minutes. Let cool.

Spread a layer of the filling on the cake and roll into a log shape.

Spread the leftover chocolate filling over the rolled cake, and use a fork to draw broken lines imitating the bark of a tree trunk. You can also decorate it with berries or other seasonal elements.

YULE SPELL

Make a spell powder charged with the energy of this holiday. Use it all year long for intentions corresponding to the festivity.

YOU WILL NEED

- Mortar and pestle
- Pine
- Cardamom
- Cinnamon
- Clove
- Cocoa powder

METHOD

Grind all the ingredients in the mortar and pestle and leave it on your altar during the Yule holiday. (You can also charge the spell powder with moonlight.) Store the mixture in glass jars for use throughout the year.

YULE CANDLES

Dress the candles (page 31) with the following elements:

- Cardamom
- Cinnamon
- Clove
- Cocoa powder

YULE RITUAL BATH

Give your guests a bottle of these salts as a gift at the end of the party, or you can make them for yourself if you are celebrating alone.

Mix the following ingredients in your mortar and pestle by the light of the full moon.

YOU WILL NEED

- Rose petals
- Marigolds
- Verbena
- 1 teaspoon cornstarch
- Ritualized coarse salt
- 1 drop of rosemary essential oil

METHOD

Add all ingredients to the bathwater and take a bath. Without rinsing yourself, get out of the bathtub and pat dry. This bath charges us with strength and magic to start the new year.

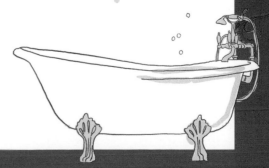

IMBOLC

FEBRUARY 1

Imbolc is a feast celebrating fertility and light and the goddess Brigid. In the Christian calendar, it's related to Saint Brigid and Candlemas. Imbolc is associated with the arrival of the lactation period of sheep symbolic of rebirth.

BRIGID'S CROSS

Brigid's cross is one of the most important symbols of this holiday. Use it to decorate your altar during Imbolc, and when the holiday is over, leave it behind the door of your home or room until the next Imbolc as a symbol of protection. Once the year has passed, replace it with a new cross and burn the old one.

METHOD

Follow the steps below, in alphabetical order. You can make it with paper or with vegetable fibers.

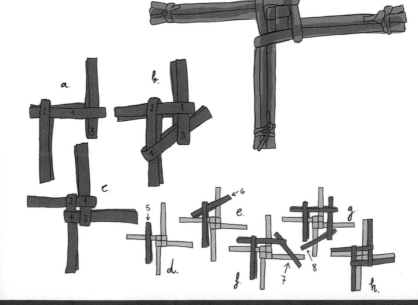

IMBOLC TRADITIONS

Here are some festive elements to inspire and guide you in how to decorate your altar or party.

FLOWERS
Iris
Plumeria
Daffodil
Rowan

HERBS
Angelica
Basil
Cinnamon

TREES
Cottonwood
Birch
Sycamore

STONES
Amethyst
Calcite
Malachite
Moonstone
Turquoise
Selenite

KEY WORDS
Awakening
Beginnings
Changes
Transition
Innocence
Patience

COLORS
Gold
White
Brown
Pink

**SYMBOLS
AND ELEMENTS**
Brigid's cross
Corn husk dolls
White candles
Brooms
Lambswool
Milk
Oheese
Potatoes
Blueberries
Strawberries
Water

DEITIES
Brigid
Gaia
Aengus Og

TAROT
Death
The Star
Strength

ANIMALS
Cow
Dragon
Sheep
Swan

**MAGICAL
INTENTION**
Astral projection
Rebirth
Birth
Cleansing
Protection
Youth

DRESS CODE

Ideally, wear brown, beige, and white hues, with details in ocher, gold, and orange. Wool is the most suitable fabric, given the direct relationship between sheep and Imbolc.

Wool is also a typical material used in making crowns with candles in honor of the goddess Brigid.

IMBOLC PARTY RECIPES

Here are some traditional recipes for this holiday. Prepare them with your guests or serve them when they arrive. If weather permits, have a picnic or celebrate in a garden.

STRAWBERRY MILKSHAKE

Strawberries

Milk or nondairy alternative

Chop the strawberries and put them in a blender. Add the milk and blend until smooth. You can also add other berries such as raspberries or blueberries.

BLUEBERRY, CHOCOLATE, AND CREAM CAKE

SERVES 12

FOR THE SPONGE CAKE:

3½ tablespoons butter

1 cup flour, sifted

¾ cup cocoa powder

4 eggs

½ cup + 2 tablespoons sugar

Vanilla extract

FOR THE FILLING:

Whipped cream

FOR THE DECORATION:

Blueberries

Whipped cream

Preheat the oven to 375°F.

In a large bowl, mix the butter with the sifted flour and cocoa powder.

Stir in the eggs, sugar, and vanilla.

Pour the batter into a greased round cake pan.

Bake for 30 minutes. Use a toothpick to test for doneness. If it comes out clean, the cake is ready.

Let cool and unmold. Cut the cake crosswise horizontally into three layers and fill with whipped cream.

Decorate the top with more whipped cream and blueberries.

IMBOLC SPELL

To end the party, you can perform this spell with your guests. You can also do it alone at your altar.

YOU WILL NEED

- 1 white candle or 1 Imbolc candle per person
- Palo santo, rosemary, or some other cleansing herb

METHOD

Use this spell to conduct an energy cleansing of your group and yourself. Have everyone light their candle. In a cauldron, light the herbs or palo santo and meditate around it while you form a circle holding hands. Feel how the smoke cleanses and purifies you.

IMBOLC CANDLES

Dress the candles (page 31) with the following elements:

- Angelica
- Basil
- Cinnamon
- Dehydrated strawberries

IMBOLC RITUAL BATH

Give your guests a bottle of this mixture as a gift at the end of the party, or you can make it for yourself if you are celebrating alone.

Mix the following ingredients in your mortar and pestle by the light of the full moon.

YOU WILL NEED

- 1 glass of milk or oat milk
- Dehydrated strawberries
- 3 drops of rose hip oil

METHOD

Add all ingredients to the bathwater and take a bath. Without rinsing yourself, get out of the bathtub and pat dry. This bath is used to attract love, abundance, and new beginnings.

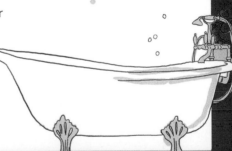

OSTARA

SPRING EQUINOX

The holiday Ostara celebrates the beginning of spring.
Certain Easter traditions originate from Ostara,
like egg painting.

OSTARA EGGS

Traditionally, we paint chicken eggs for decoration, alluding to birth, beginnings, and new opportunities. You can cook them beforehand (in which case they'd spoil quickly) or paint them raw (first empty the shell by carefully pricking it with a needle, and then draining the contents). You can draw a pattern or motif on a separate sheet of paper before painting the egg. Here's a template for drawing the first one.

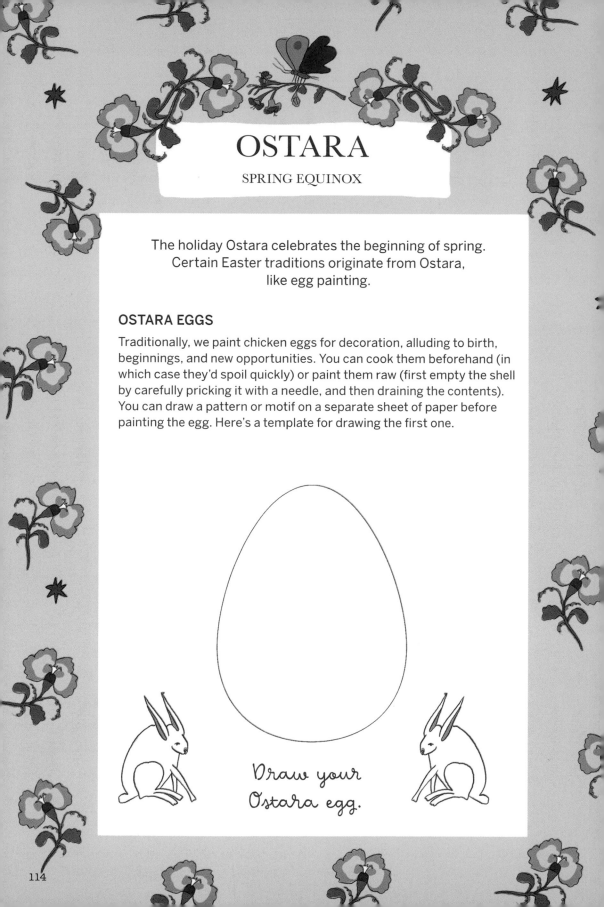

*Draw your
Ostara egg.*

OSTARA TRADITIONS

Here are some festive elements to inspire and guide you in how to decorate your altar or party.

FLOWERS
Daisy
Tulip
Violet
Jasmine
Lilac

HERBS
Lemongrass
Spearmint
Mint
Retama

TREES
Apple
Orange
Lemon

STONES
Agate
Aquamarine
Aventurine
Citrine
Jade
Ruby

KEY WORDS
Balance
Birth
Change
Love
Beginnings
Fertility

COLORS
Green
Light blue
Pink
Silver
White

SYMBOLS AND ELEMENTS
Baskets
Eggs
Butterflies
Seeds
Asparagus
Honey
Radishes
Spring cleaning
Handicrafts
Gardening

TAROT
The Empress
Justice
The Star

ANIMALS
Bees
Butterflies
Chicks
Rabbit
Phoenix

MAGICAL INTENTION
Love
Lust
Abundance
Balance
Growth
Passion

DRESS CODE

It's similar to Beltane, but we can differentiate it by wearing pastel colors and matching flower crowns.

FLOWER CROWN

Follow these illustrations to make your own flower crown.

OSTARA PARTY RECIPES

Here are some traditional recipes for this holiday. Prepare them with your guests or serve them when they arrive. Ideally, have a picnic or celebrate in a garden.

GRASSHOPPER COCKTAIL

Crushed ice

1 ounce crème de menthe

1 ounce crème de cacao

2 ounces heavy cream

Mix all ingredients well in a blender or shaker.

Serve very cold.

SCRAMBLED EGGS WITH ASPARAGUS

SERVES 4

20 spears asparagus

Extra-virgin olive oil

6 eggs

Salt

Pepper

Fresh herbs (optional)

4 slices rye bread, for serving

Butter

Cut the asparagus into small pieces.

Heat a drizzle of oil in a pan. Sauté the asparagus and set aside.

Beat the eggs until smooth, then sprinkle with salt, pepper, and herbs, if using. Stir in the asparagus.

Heat a drizzle of oil in a pan. Add the egg mixture. Cook over very low heat, stirring constantly, until the eggs are cooked through but still soft.

Toast each slice of rye bread with a dab of butter in a frying pan.

Serve the eggs on top of the toast, seasoned with salt and pepper to taste.

OSTARA SPELL: RITUAL OF THE SEEDS

Asking for a seed blessing is a very simple ritual to drive forward a new project, stage, or relationship. The seeds represent your project.

YOU WILL NEED

- Seeds
- 1 shovel
- Soil (either from your garden or from a pot)

METHOD

Choose an outdoor spot to plant your seeds. Ask nature, or your favorite goddess, to bless the seeds so that they can become a plant that will grow strong. Take care of them daily.

OSTARA CANDLES

Dress the candles (page 31) with the following elements:

- Spearmint
- Daisy
- Violet petals
- Jasmine essential oil

OSTARA RITUAL BATH

Give your guests a bottle of these salts as a gift at the end of the party, or you can make them for yourself if you are celebrating alone.

Mix the following ingredients in your mortar and pestle by the light of the full moon.

YOU WILL NEED

- Rose petals
- Spearmint
- Daisy
- Violet petals
- 2 drops of jasmine essential oil
- Ritualized coarse salt
- 1 capful of Florida water

METHOD

Add all ingredients to the bathwater and take a bath. Without rinsing yourself, get out of the bathtub and pat dry. This bath serves to start a new project, stage, or relationship with positive energy and is also an energy cleanse.

Tradition, Wicca, and eclecticism in magical festivals

These holidays you just read about are celebrated by neopagans, Wiccans, witches, and people who simply seek this beautiful and special connection with nature.

They give us time to pause, connect with nature, celebrate magic, and honor family traditions and rituals.

There are more gods, plants, recipes, rituals, and traditions associated with each festival, just as each tradition can vary and have different nuances in each town, country, and culture. I have tried to provide you with the basics so that you can begin to create your own rituals, recipes, and traditions associated with each holiday. Keep a record of them in your grimoire.

8.
ASTROLOGY APPLIED TO MAGIC

In this chapter, you'll learn which astrological tools to use when performing certain rituals. You'll also find a summary of the energy of each sign, the importance of the moon and its phases, and much more. If you want to go deeper into the astrological chart, planets, signs, myths, or compatibilities (among other topics), my first book, *Signs of the Zodiac*, offers a very complete illustrated guide to astrology.

THE ENERGY OF

ARIES

Associated with initiative, passion, beginnings, impulses, war, aggressiveness, individualism, leadership, spontaneity, entrepreneurship, directness, pioneering, explosiveness, impatience, and honesty.

TAURUS

Associated with stability, patience, elegance, materialism, kindness, certainty, delicacy, stubbornness, optimism, sensuality, practicality, realism, possessiveness, selfishness, and generosity.

GEMINI

Associated with agitation, communication, duality, instability, intellectuality, versatility, imagination, logic, shrewdness, mental acuity, and restlessness.

CANCER

Associated with kindness, sensitivity, affection, home, intuition, emotional intelligence, family, empathy, emotional instability, fickleness, harmony, discretion, gentleness, protection, reserve, and mystery.

LEO

Associated with affection, passion, assertiveness, charisma, competitiveness, courage, egocentrism, excesses, frankness, festivity, generosity, interest, narcissism, pride, joviality, and enjoyment.

VIRGO

Associated with analysis, calmness, kindness, criticism, the need for control, neatness, order, honesty, strategy, austerity, perfectionism, logic, rationality, caution, and precaution.

EACH ZODIAC SIGN

LIBRA

Associated with balance and the search for it, beauty, culture, calmness, assertiveness, extravagance, elegance, seduction, persuasion, harmony, indecision, romanticism, and vanity.

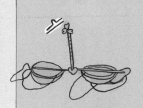

SCORPIO

Associated with passion, hidden intentions, control, jealousy, obsession, sex, death, intuition, determination, magnetism, mystery, reserve, caution, and revenge.

SAGITTARIUS

Associated with travel, extroversion, philosophy, joy, adventure, brusqueness, good humor, cosmopolitanism, curiosity, enthusiasm, generosity, insight, and impatience.

CAPRICORN

Associated with authority, ambition, arrogance, conservatism, tradition, pragmatism, reserve, fortitude, exigency, responsibility, resilience, leadership, intransigence, and fulfillment of duty.

AQUARIUS

Associated with innovation, the disruptive, the different, mental agility, creativity, philanthropy, independence, freedom, rigor, provocation, insight, sociability, revolution, and logic.

PISCES

Associated with emotion, art, sensitivity, empathy, music, spirituality, creativity, kindness, fear, idealism, attentiveness, serenity, intuition, and magic.

Below you will find a guide to the best time to do a ritual or spell. It's not set in stone; you can do many rituals at any time, but it's important to keep in mind the following:

- The general astral climate (what planets are in which signs, if any are retrograde, or if there's an eclipse)
- Time correspondences (the hours and days related to each planet)
- The moon (the sign and phase are the most relevant markers, as we will see)

HOURLY CORRESPONDENCES
The day and time for your spells

		SUNDAY	MONDAY	TUESDAY	WEDNESDAY	THURSDAY	FRIDAY	SATURDAY
(MIDNIGHT TO NOON)	1.	Sun	Moon	Mars	Mercury	Jupiter	Venus	Saturn
	2.	Venus	Saturn	Sun	Moon	Mars	Mercury	Jupiter
	3.	Mercury	Jupiter	Venus	Saturn	Sun	Moon	Mars
	4.	Moon	Mars	Mercury	Jupiter	Venus	Saturn	Sun
	5.	Saturn	Sun	Moon	Mars	Mercury	Jupiter	Venus
	6.	Jupiter	Venus	Saturn	Sun	Moon	Mars	Mercury
	7.	Mars	Mercury	Jupiter	Venus	Saturn	Sun	Moon
	8.	Sun	Moon	Mars	Mercury	Jupiter	Venus	Saturn
	9.	Venus	Saturn	Sun	Moon	Mars	Mercury	Jupiter
	10.	Mercury	Jupiter	Venus	Saturn	Sun	Moon	Mars
	11.	Moon	Mars	Mercury	Jupiter	Venus	Saturn	Sun
	12.	Saturn	Sun	Moon	Mars	Mercury	Jupiter	Venus
(NOON TO MIDNIGHT)	1.	Jupiter	Venus	Saturn	Sun	Moon	Mars	Mercury
	2.	Mars	Mercury	Jupiter	Venus	Saturn	Sun	Moon
	3.	Sun	Moon	Mars	Mercury	Jupiter	Venus	Saturn
	4.	Venus	Saturn	Sun	Moon	Mars	Mercury	Jupiter
	5.	Mercury	Jupiter	Venus	Saturn	Sun	Moon	Mars
	6.	Moon	Mars	Mercury	Jupiter	Venus	Saturn	Sun
	7.	Saturn	Sun	Moon	Mars	Mercury	Jupiter	Venus
	8.	Jupiter	Venus	Saturn	Sun	Moon	Mars	Mercury
	9.	Mars	Mercury	Jupiter	Venus	Saturn	Sun	Moon
	10.	Sun	Moon	Mars	Mercury	Jupiter	Venus	Saturn
	11.	Venus	Saturn	Sun	Moon	Mars	Mercury	Jupiter
	12.	Mercury	Jupiter	Venus	Saturn	Sun	Moon	Mars

Following traditional astrology, the planet that corresponds to the first hour of the day is also the one that corresponds to the day in question. A planet can be the main planet of the day and of the hour, in which case the timing of the ritual will be doubly appropriate according to the intention related to the planet.

Sun: beginnings, starts.
Moon: emotional stability, psychic energy, intuition, mysteries.
Mars: action, sex, initiative, activation, opening of roads, dispute resolution.

Mercury: communication, business.
Jupiter: luck, expansion.
Venus: love, attraction, beauty.
Saturn: work, limits, effort, self-improvement.

The Moon!

The moon is the celestial body most directly related to magic. When choosing the right time for our rituals, we must consider the moon's phase and in what sign it is located, as well as if it's off course or if it has a complicated relationship with a planet (find more on planetary aspects in *Signs of the Zodiac*). Even so, astrology does not force you to choose a specific moment in time; it signals the most appropriate one, but that doesn't mean it's the only one.

THE FULL MOONS OF THE YEAR

Names and correspondences may vary from place to place;
these are my favorites.

JANUARY
Name: Wolf Moon
Colors: white, blue
Theme: beginnings

FEBRUARY
Name: Snow Moon
Colors: white, black
Theme: purification

MARCH
Name: Worm Moon
Colors: green, white
Theme: prosperity

APRIL
Name: Pink Moon
Color: pink
Theme: growth

MAY
Name: Flower Moon
Colors: green, pink, blue
Themes: love, well-being

JUNE
Name: Strawberry Moon
Colors: red, pink
Themes: abundance, prosperity, love

JULY
Name: Buck Moon
Colors: yellow, orange
Themes: strength, labor

AUGUST
Name: Sturgeon Moon
Colors: white, yellow
Themes: evolution, growth

SEPTEMBER
Name: Corn Moon
Colors: green, yellow
Theme: home

OCTOBER
Name: Hunter Moon
Colors: purple, black
Themes: cleansing, ancestors

NOVEMBER
Name: Beaver Moon
Color: white
Themes: healing, protection

DECEMBER
Name: Cold Moon
Colors: white, black
Themes: peace, strength, rebirth

LUNAR PHASES

New Moon

Crescent Moon

Waning Moon

Crescent Quarter

Waning Quarter

Waning Gibbous

Growing Gibbous

Full Moon

- **New Moon:** beginnings, planting seeds, wiping the slate clean, rebirth.
- **Crescent Moon:** new energy, desire, motivation, small steps, making plans to achieve your goals.
- **Crescent Quarter:** strength, fertility, attraction, work, energy.
- **Growing Gibbous:** patience, growth, preparation.
- **Full Moon:** fullness, manifestation, energy, healing, power, results.
- **Waning Gibbous:** rebalancing, seeking harmony, energy cleansing.
- **Waning Quarter:** deep cleansing, getting rid of blockages, cutting ties with harmful situations or people.
- **Waning Moon:** self-care, reflection, meditation, patience, rendition.

NEW MOON

This is the first phase of the lunar cycle. The moon is completely dark and does not reflect any light, so it is the ideal time to pay attention to our senses, be comfortable in our space, and rest our mind and body.

KEY WORDS

Beginning, darkness, interior, inquiry, renewal, introspection, creation, starting over, new opportunity.

RITUALS

- Connect with the darkness. Spend time alone, self-reflect, and keep a journal.
- Plant the seeds for what you want to achieve; visualize yourself as if you already have it (we'll cover manifestation in chapter 10).
- Drink an infusion of herbs that are related to clarity and intuition: rosemary, sage, yarrow.
- Write a letter to your future self. Make a list of what you want to manifest or achieve in the next twenty-eight days of the lunar cycle.
- Track your emotions and their relationship to the moon; write them down in a journal.
- Pay attention to your magical space. If you don't have one, or want to reorganize it, now is a good time.
- Clean your magical space (this can also be done during a waning moon).
- Take a cleansing bath (you'll find several recipes throughout the book).
- Let go: Visualize what no longer serves you, write it down, and destroy the paper. Feel how you free yourself from it.

NOTE:

Some people prefer not to do rituals on the new moon because it's said that many witches who use black magic do their rituals then. That is why it's better to dedicate the new moon to rest and introspection and leave the cleansing rituals for the waning moon. It's not advisable to cut your hair in this lunar phase.

CRESCENT MOON

This is the second lunar phase. It's time to take action, align ourselves with our purposes, make positive affirmations, get to work, and execute plans and intentions.

KEY WORDS
Process, creation, work, growth, progress, optimism, facing challenges, opening paths, attraction.

RITUALS
- Rituals aimed at attracting abundance and economic prosperity (page 190).
- Rituals aimed at attracting love (page 188).
- Road-opening rituals (page 190).
- Rituals of success.
- Start new projects or businesses (take a good look at the astral climate before doing so).
- Decision making.
- Manifest what you desire or make things happen (page 194).
- Set intentions and carry out the action to make them happen.
- Good time to charge tarot cards, crystals, or minerals.
- Good time to enhance your gifts and virtues.

NOTE:
This is a good phase to cut your hair so that it grows fast and not ideal for waxing or shaving because the hair will grow in sooner.

FULL MOON

This is the phase that is most related to magic and witches. It's very powerful. The moon is fully illuminated. It's the most magical time of the lunar cycle.

KEY WORDS
Epitome, wholeness, energy, movement, gratitude, celebration, meditation, self-care, beauty, connection.

RITUALS
- Charge your crystals, tarot cards, oracles, amulets, and any other magical objects in the moonlight.
- Rituals of beauty and self-love.
- Take an Aphrodite salt bath (page 188).
- Take care of yourself, pamper yourself, meditate.
- Throw tarot cards for self-knowledge and self-exploration, and keep a diary of your emotions.
- Make a list of the things you are grateful for.
- Let your energy flow through movement.

NOTE:
This is the best time to cut your hair so that it grows healthy, strong, and shiny, especially if you do it between six and twelve o'clock in the morning.

Most women menstruate during this lunar phase. During the full moon, some people can feel very tired and even get headaches; if so, take a break. On the other hand, others feel invigorated and energized; if this is you, take advantage of this opportunity to celebrate and socialize. Do what resonates with you.

It's said that if you have sex during the full moon while you are menstruating, and your intention is to bind the person you are with to you, it will be one of the most powerful love moorings that exist. It's also said to have very dangerous consequences. But if you do it unintentionally or unknowingly, it is not dangerous and nothing will happen.

WANING MOON

This is the last phase, where the moon is becoming less visible and is associated with rituals of cleansing and anything related to expelling something from our life. It also helps destroy negative energies or spells that may have been cast on us.

KEY WORDS

Cleansing, banishment, expulsion, diminishment, driving away, destruction.

RITUALS

- Energy cleansing of your magical space, people, yourself, or situations.
- Turning rituals to return to others the evil they may have wished on us (page 192).
- Rituals to break a toxic bond we may have with a person (page 193).
- Rituals to get rid of bad habits.
- Let go and release what no longer serves your purpose.
- Throw away physical objects that you no longer need; clean and tidy your space, both your magical one and your room or home.
- End a relationship (work, romantic, friendship) that you feel is no longer aligned with you.
- Initiate detox diets.

NOTE:

This is not a good phase to cut your hair, as it will grow more slowly and will be weaker. However, it's a good phase for shaving or waxing, precisely for the same reason.

MOON IN ARIES

The Moon in the Signs

Rituals related to leadership, courage, bravery, and willpower. It's time to start something, to trust yourself and show what you're worth.

Candle color: burgundy red.   **Crystals:** ruby, red jasper.   **Element:** fire.

NEW MOON IN ARIES

Favorable moon to start new projects and feel deserving of everything good, knowing we have the necessary power and strength. Focus your energy to go all out during the crescent moon.

CRESCENT MOON IN ARIES

Good time to bet on our courage, strength, and power. Related to the energy of the warrior, we can overcome anything and move forward with determination and strength toward our goals.

FULL MOON IN ARIES

Celebrate our strength, initiative, and courage through ritual. Or take advantage of the full moon to feel powerful and like a leader through a ritual or meditation.

WANING MOON IN ARIES

Very powerful moon for removing obstacles, impediments, and hindrances to our personal growth, and for finding the necessary strength and drive typical of Aries.

MOON IN TAURUS

The Moon in the Signs

Rituals related to beauty, pleasure, love, sensuality, prosperity, self-esteem, and self-love.

Candle colors: green, pink.   **Crystals:** rose quartz, sapphire.   **Element:** earth.

NEW MOON IN TAURUS

Good phase to initiate work projects, acquire new properties, or start a romance. I don't recommend doing complex rituals during this phase; focus on simple rituals with the above themes.

CRESCENT MOON IN TAURUS

Rituals related to beauty, work, Aphrodite, beauty elixirs, or attraction. Good time for rituals related to abundance and attraction in business and romance.

FULL MOON IN TAURUS

Splendid moment to perform a powerful ritual of attraction. To have strength and courage in relation to pleasure. To celebrate ourselves and all that we have achieved, and to treat ourselves to something special.

WANING MOON IN TAURUS

Do simple cleanses with this moon. We should do rituals on this moon only if we want to move something in a drastic way (from a theoretical point of view, but always follow your intuition).

MOON IN GEMINI

The Moon in the Signs

Rituals related to communication and adaptation to new circumstances, or rituals related to our social skills and social life.

Candle color: yellow.   **Crystals:** tiger's eye, amber.   **Element:** air.

NEW MOON IN GEMINI

Planting the seeds or laying the groundwork for an intellectual (such as writing a novel) or academic (a thesis) project, and focusing the energy to work on them as they grow. Ideal time to plan trips, relocations, or moves.

CRESCENT MOON IN GEMINI

Rituals focused on mental clarity, truth, and effective communication. It's also a good time to do rituals related to improving social skills or public speaking.

FULL MOON IN GEMINI

This moon is one of the best for launching an intellectual project (novel, thesis, dissertation), so that it can be disseminated and gain interest among the public and critics. Pay attention to the messages hidden in dreams and intuitions.

WANING MOON IN GEMINI

This is the time to drive away negative thoughts, clear up misunderstandings, and resolve everything that prevents clear and accurate communication.

MOON IN CANCER

The Moon in the Signs

The moon rules this sign; therefore, this is the time to honor the goddesses related to the moon and perform rituals related to home, family, and fertility.

Candle color: white.   **Crystals:** moonstone, opal.   **Element:** water.

NEW MOON IN CANCER

Fertility rituals (to become pregnant) or beginning rituals related to the home, such as buying a new house or welcoming a new family member, such as a pet.

CRESCENT MOON IN CANCER

Rituals focused on strengthening and improving the relationship between different members of our family, family harmony, and the atmosphere at home.

FULL MOON IN CANCER

The most successful ritual in this phase of the moon is related to protecting your home, your magical space, and your family.

WANING MOON IN CANCER

A time to work with feminine energy, to take care of ourselves, to collect ourselves, to perform an energy cleansing, and to connect with the moon and our feminine and intuitive parts.

MOON IN LEO

The Moon in the Signs

Rituals related to personal value, creativity, self-confidence and the power within, success, and triumph. If you want to feel more confident and empowered, this is the best moon to work with.

Candle colors: yellow, gold.   **Crystals:** tiger's eye, citrine.   **Element:** fire.

NEW MOON IN LEO

The best moon to "inaugurate" a personal and creative project, asking for it to go well and performing some kind of ritual to make it a success. Also a time to initiate a new stage of confidence.

CRESCENT MOON IN LEO

This moon is ideal for enhancing our personal attractiveness, charisma, and leadership skills. If you have a business or creative project, perform rituals to keep it on a successful track.

FULL MOON IN LEO

The best time to perform a powerful ritual of self-love, self-esteem, and self-confidence to improve our self-perception, and, therefore, to make others find us more attractive.

WANING MOON IN LEO

The perfect phase to remove people from our lives who do not value us, and to cut ties with anything that prevents us from succeeding, either directly or through a ritual.

MOON IN VIRGO

The Moon in the Signs

Rituals related to work, routine, service, offering the best
of yourself, healing, improving your habits and daily routine,
and being more consistent and organized.

Candle color: blue.   **Crystals:** lapis lazuli, malachite.   **Element:** earth.

NEW MOON IN VIRGO

Rituals in this phase of the moon require a lot of concentration and
meticulousness. It's the right time to draw up a new plan that will help
you be more organized.

CRESCENT MOON IN VIRGO

This is an ideal moon to focus our efforts on helping others and
understanding them better, even for therapists. Rituals to focus on
empathy and service to others.

FULL MOON IN VIRGO

This is a perfect moon for very elaborate and complex rituals, where
neatness and accuracy are necessary. Also for activities that require
the aforementioned characteristics.

WANING MOON IN VIRGO

It's the best time to remove obstacles that prevent us from thriving in
our work life. Also to remove jealousy, envy, and other negative
feelings and energies.

MOON IN LIBRA

The Moon in the Signs

Rituals related to aesthetics, harmony, beauty, balance, legal problems, associations, and sentimental relationships.

Candle color: pink.   **Crystals:** rose quartz, jade.   **Element:** air.

NEW MOON IN LIBRA

A good time to start a new artistic stage, open an exhibition, and present a fashion collection, or any project related to art and design.

CRESCENT MOON IN LIBRA

Rituals focused on creating healthy, strong, and lasting relationships, especially in love, but also in the workplace.

FULL MOON IN LIBRA

The best moon for powerful rituals of beauty, love, desire, and attraction, for finding our inner peace and balance, and for harmonious relationships.

WANING MOON IN LIBRA

A good phase to keep injustices away from us and to settle anything legal related. Rituals focused on resolving complicated situations.

MOON IN SCORPIO

The Moon in the Signs

This is one of the most powerful and intense moons, so it's appropriate for issues related to love, sexuality, the occult, changes, transformation, and so on. This moon is especially related to the world of magic.

Candle colors: red, black.   **Crystals:** onyx, tourmaline.   **Element:** water.

NEW MOON IN SCORPIO

An appropriate moon to define new objectives, especially related to the emotional world, and particularly to end a painful stage and start over with a clean slate.

CRESCENT MOON IN SCORPIO

Perfect moon to get rid of obsessive or toxic patterns in our relationships, as long as our will is firm.

FULL MOON IN SCORPIO

Very powerful moon to make a big change, to end a transformative process, or to charge us with energy so we are able to carry out this huge shift.

WANING MOON IN SCORPIO

Moon related to the world of tarot, divination, mediums, and intuition. Rituals to enhance these virtues or to perform these activities.

MOON IN SAGITTARIUS

The Moon in the Signs

Rituals related to expansion, travel, fun, curiosity,
and spiritual quest.

Candle colors: blue, purple.   **Crystal:** topaz.   **Element:** fire.

NEW MOON IN SAGITTARIUS

It's time to consider what activities related to spirituality speak to us
and which of them we'd like to start. Tarot, yoga, astrology . . .

CRESCENT MOON IN SAGITTARIUS

Perfect time for rituals related to good luck. Also for rituals focused on
spiritual connection and tapping into our intuition and psychic gifts.

FULL MOON IN SAGITTARIUS

Ideal moon to do a guided meditation, yoga, or some ritual of good luck
or one related to connecting with the world and opening our horizons.

WANING MOON IN SAGITTARIUS

This is a good moon to break blockages, do physical and energy
cleansing, and get rid of insecurities that prevent us from advancing in
our spiritual awakening.

MOON IN CAPRICORN

The Moon in the Signs

Rituals related to economy, labor, abundance, economic prosperity, determination, strength, self-confidence, ambition, and having a clear and calm mind.

Candle color: brown.   **Crystals:** onyx, smoky quartz.   **Element:** earth.

NEW MOON IN CAPRICORN

This is a good lunar phase to plan our professional goals and objectives and create an action plan to achieve them throughout the lunar cycle. These can be short-, medium-, or long-term plans.

CRESCENT MOON IN CAPRICORN

This is the best moon to perform rituals for achieving our goals and improving our work life.

FULL MOON IN CAPRICORN

The best time to do a powerful ritual of abundance, economy, or self-confidence.

WANING MOON IN CAPRICORN

It's a good phase for an energy cleanse and to get rid of both personal insecurities and economic blockages.

MOON IN AQUARIUS

The Moon in the Signs

Rituals related to community, social impact and influence, creativity, innovation, revolution, disruption, and freedom.

Candle color: blue.   **Crystals:** turquoise, fluorite.   **Element:** air.

NEW MOON IN AQUARIUS

In this phase the affirmations should revolve around feeling freer, lighter, and unattached to develop our potential to the fullest.

CRESCENT MOON IN AQUARIUS

This phase is appropriate to attract a major change in any area of our life: social, romantic, economic. And especially to obtain a broader social life or more friendships.

FULL MOON IN AQUARIUS

This is a wonderful moon to enhance freedom, agility, and lucidity. Immerse yourself in the energy of this time if you want to feel freer, more rational, and original in your ideas and actions.

WANING MOON IN AQUARIUS

It's the best moon to free ourselves from blockages and situations, as well as relationships that restrict our personal freedom or limit our future.

MOON IN PISCES

The Moon in the Signs

Rituals related to inspiration, psychic abilities, intuition, creativity, empathy, emotional management, dreams, and idealism.

Candle colors: blue, green.　**Crystals:** angelite, aquamarine.　**Element:** water.

NEW MOON IN PISCES

This is a perfect moon to visualize our dreams and project them into the future with vibrations of abundance (in chapter 10 you'll find more information about abundance rituals).

CRESCENT MOON IN PISCES

Ideal lunar phase to connect with our intuitive and spiritual sides and to grow and improve in these aspects.

FULL MOON IN PISCES

It's magical, emotional, intuitive, and one of the most powerful moons. Perfect for working on our connection with the universe and our spiritual and psychic gifts.

WANING MOON IN PISCES

The best phase for resting and for strengthening our "emotional armor" so that the vibrations and emotions of others do not affect us negatively.

141

MOON WATER

Water charged with moonlight absorbs its elements and has many magical uses. Depending on the sign and phase of the moon, moon water will have different properties.

HOW IS MOON WATER MADE?

Leave a clear glass bottle, filled with water, in the moonlight and pick It up before dawn. Do not put a stopper on it; use a cloth or gauze to cover the mouth of the bottle.

PROPERTIES OF MOON WATER ACCORDING TO PHASE

- **New Moon:** There is no moonlight, and therefore no moon water is made in this phase.

- **Crescent Moon:** This moon water is related to growth, empowerment, and attraction. It is used in rituals with these themes.

- **Full Moon:** It's the most popular and powerful moon water. Charged by the light of this moon, it will be full of magical energy, related to the sign where it's found.

- **Waning Moon:** It's best for cleansing and purifying.

MOON WATER USES

- Cleansing
- Infusions and coffee
- Rituals and spells
- Watering plants

FREQUENTLY ASKED QUESTIONS

Q: Does it have to be left overnight?
A: No, three or four hours is enough.

Q: Can the sun shine on it?
A: It's best to store it in a place where it's not directly exposed to sunlight.

THE LUNAR CYCLE AND MENSTRUAL CYCLE

MENSTRUATION
New Moon

Crescent Moon

Waning Moon

OVULATION
Full Moon

- The lunar cycle and the average menstrual cycle have the same length (twenty-nine days). The word *menstruation* comes from the Latin *mensis* (month) and the Greek word *mene* (moon).

- The wise old woman (menstruation, new moon): meditation, tranquility, rest, slowing down.

- The maiden (preovulatory phase, crescent moon): organization, productivity, high energy levels.

- The mother (ovulation, full moon): increased sexual desire, attraction, affection.

- The sorceress (premenstrual phase, waning moon): loneliness, spiritual connection, adjustments in our timing.

OTHER ASTROLOGICAL ASPECTS

ECLIPSES

It's usually best not to perform rituals during eclipses, because the energy is disturbed and very powerful; instead, let's just go with the flow unless you control magic well or have a strong instinct that it would be a good time for a particular ritual.

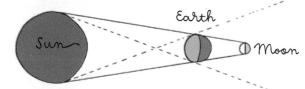

Lunar Eclipse

A lunar eclipse only happens on a full moon.

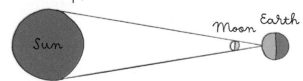

Solar Eclipse

A solar eclipse only happens on a new moon.

RETROGRADES

Some witches say that it's better not to cast spells when Mercury, Venus, or Mars is retrograde (or even other planets). Others don't see this as an issue if your intention is clear and firm. Do what resonates with you.

ASTRAL CLIMATE

Before launching a project, check where the planets are located. The best time is with the sun in a fire sign, with good aspects in Jupiter, Venus, and Saturn.

9.
DIVINATION

Different practices of divination appear in all cultures. They are used to foresee future events, to understand what another person feels, wishes, or thinks, or to acknowledge past, present, and future situations. Some tools, such as tarot, are also useful for introspection and self-exploration. Other divination methods help us receive messages from alternate planes of reality.

Below is a list of the most common tools you can use when it comes to divination. Follow your intuition when it comes to which tool to choose, as well as my general guidance on the following pages.

- Tarot cards
- Crystal ball
- Pendulum
- Runes
- Palm reading
- Tasseomancy (reading tea leaves)
- Ceromancy (reading melted wax)
- Ouija

TAROT

WHAT IS TAROT?

It is a deck of seventy-eight cards (twenty-two major arcana and fifty-six minor arcana) that is traditionally used for divination.

MAJOR AND MINOR ARCANA

The major arcana are twenty-two cards that represent archetypes; that is, general concepts of human life with a profound message. They carry their own name, the first card being the Fool (arcana 0) and the last, the World (arcana 21). We will look at these twenty-two cards in detail in the following pages. In a spread, the majors contain important messages, put into context by the minors. Some tarot readers use only the majors to throw their cards. If you're just starting out, this is a good way to begin, as it's simpler.

The minor arcana are similar to a deck of playing cards in that they have four suits or families (wands, cups, swords, pentacles). Each suit symbolizes a different theme. In my tarot, the Tarot de Carlotydes, each suit follows a different chromatic range to aid in interpretation. In the Tarot de Marseille, one of the classic tarots, the minor arcana are represented similarly to playing cards. The majors have an elaborate illustration; on the other hand, the drawing of the minors is simpler, representing the elements of the card (for example, the drawing on the three of wands is simply three wands, nothing more). The first deck to include more complex illustrations, attempting to explain the card's meaning, was the Rider-Waite Tarot, illustrated by the artist Pamela Colman Smith and published in 1910. Since then, great artists such as Salvador Dalí and Leonora Carrington have created their own versions of tarot decks. Illustrators and artists today, including myself, have also created their own tarot decks. Mine, the Tarot de Carlotydes, contains seventy-eight arcana, based on the classic tarot decks, but I have created a new system that speeds up and simplifies learning. On the following pages you will see the illustrations of the major arcana.

You can read the cards as they appear in the spread, taking into account whether they look at us or not (if they are upright or reversed) or only paying attention to the meaning of the card positioned on the right of the spread—whatever resonates with you. They can also be read by interpreting that an upside-down or reversed card has the same meaning as the card that is upright and looks at us, but the message and energy of the card is blocked or has difficulty manifesting itself.

Upright Card   Reversed Card

WHAT DO YOU NEED TO START LEARNING TAROT?

- A deck that you like: It doesn't matter what it is, but you must feel attracted to it; it should speak to you and you should connect with it. You could go with the Rider-Waite deck, my own, or that of another artist you like. You can also have more than one deck and collect them.

- A tarot diary: This is a notebook to write down everything you learn.

- Patience: Start little by little. Connect with the energy of each card one at a time, study them, and start with simple spreads.

- Develop your intuition and connect with your deck: Trust your instinct, the sensations that the cards transmit to you. Connect with the deck by keeping it in your magical space or in a special place, touching it, looking at the cards, or even sleeping with them.

- Clean and charge the deck: Just as with any other magical tool, you must clean its energy when you acquire it (you don't need to get it as a gift; you can buy it yourself). Charge it to activate it and let it absorb your energy (see chapter 5). Also make sure to clean it once you're done throwing the cards.

- A purple mat: It can be another color, but purple is related to magic and intuition. When throwing the cards, use the mat to highlight the space.

- A white or purple candle: A candle will help you distinguish the moment and connect with the universe, and your intuition.

THE MAJOR ARCANA

0. THE FOOL

This card is related to the element fire, but also to the set of the four elements. It's considered the arcana 0 or 22, depending on the system that is followed. I consider it the 0 because the Fool symbolizes potential, the journey of life. The Fool is the starting arcana, the daring one. Spontaneity, innocence, and youthful strength are concepts that this card encompasses. On the more negative side are recklessness, imprudence, and taking unnecessary risks.

When interpreting this card, we must consider not only the meaning of the card but also that of the cards surrounding it in the spread and how they relate to one another.

UPRIGHT MEANING

In a spread, it indicates a beginning, a piece of advice, to take the plunge, to dare, to bet on adventure, on a less rational and more innocent approach. It may speak to us of the vital energy of teenagers, who are simply eager to begin, to dive headfirst to explore. It may want to tell us to connect with that part of ourselves, with the wild, the rebellious. It can also generally speak to us of a new stage that we begin with excitement of undertakings.

In love, it indicates a fun relationship, but not a serious commitment. At work, your ideas may be seen as a bit crazy, too innovative for most people. In money, it is a good card, a new source of unexpected income, for example. Spiritually, it signals a new learning path.

REVERSED MEANING

The inverted meaning of the card speaks to us of having unwise attitudes that can harm us. There may be possible deception, and someone may be taking advantage of your naïveté. Also, it can indicate that you are being too short-sighted and you should plan more for the future, that your lifestyle is somewhat chaotic and is not benefiting you, that you are facing instability or problems with issues such as freedom or independence.

1. THE MAGICIAN

This is related to the element air, specifically to the planet Mercury, which is the ruler of Virgo and Gemini. It's considered arcana 1. The Magician is the arcana that speaks of our logical and intellectual resources—our mental capacity to move our projects or ideas forward, connecting the intellectual capacity, the tools, and the results.

When interpreting it, we must consider not only the meaning of the card but also that of the cards surrounding it in the spread and how they relate to one another.

UPRIGHT MEANING

In a spread, it indicates good, proactive energy, related to willpower and the ability to make our dreams come true. The message will revolve around taking advantage of the resources at your disposal through your intelligence to realize those desires. It has much more to do with the mind than with the emotions, so it will usually relay issues related to work or material resources. If the Magician appears in a spread related to love, it may indicate a beneficial relationship on a practical level, or that your person of interest is very determined and logical. If you are looking for love, it may be a favorable time; you will take advantage of the opportunities that arise.

REVERSED MEANING

The reversed meaning of the card tells us there's a chance we're being manipulated; we could have doubts or be insecure about our qualities or the person we're asking about. It can also indicate that we're distracted, we have a lack of mental clarity, we do not have clear objectives and, therefore, we're wasting opportunities. It invites us to put our mind in order and see that resources may be right there, even if we're not aware of them at the moment.

2. THE HIGH PRIESTESS

This is card number 2 and it's related to the element water. This card speaks of intuition, wisdom, spirituality, and sensitivity, traditionally considered feminine. It also speaks of the subconscious, our inner voice, and the spiritual guide that shows us the way in times of crisis. It's one of the cards with the most feminine energy, focused on the spiritual and sensitive side.

When interpreting it, we must consider not only the meaning of the card but also that of the cards surrounding it in the spread and how they relate to one another.

UPRIGHT MEANING

In a spread, it indicates sensitivity, spirituality, and wisdom. It's also related to femininity, to mothers, to motherhood. If we ask about a person, it can also indicate something mysterious about them. It may be a wise person but doesn't easily reveal them, instead keeping that knowledge as a valuable treasure.

In love, this card can suggest a very magical and even spiritual connection. But it also notes that the other person (especially if it's a woman) is out of reach or unknown to the person who's asking. If you are a woman, it indicates that you have a magical and mysterious appeal.

At work, it's a good card; you have a good position, but it invites you to observe and not to reveal everything you know.

REVERSED MEANING

When the High Priestess card appears inverted, we focus on the negative side of the card: hidden intentions, people who may be doing things that can harm you without your knowledge. It's also an invitation to listen to your inner voice and focus on yourself to discover your truth.

3. THE EMPRESS

This is card number 3 and it's related to the element air, the planet Venus, and the signs Taurus and Libra (although Justice usually represents Libra).

The Empress speaks of faith, but from a feminist point of view. It portrays a woman who is confident, with clear priorities, and who performs her duties to perfection. It's also somewhat mysterious and subtle and related to feminine sexual energy.

When interpreting it, we must consider not only the meaning of the card but also that of the cards surrounding it in the spread and how they relate to one another.

UPRIGHT MEANING

This is a card that can speak of a woman (or yourself if you're consulting and you're a woman) who is considered valuable and is attractive to others because she is confident. It also speaks of sharing our knowledge and being open to helping others, based on our own experience. In love, it speaks to us of a full, secure love. You will feel attractive and will attract others because of your self-assuredness and calmness. At work, it speaks of stability and how others perceive you as a wise, committed, and decisive person.

REVERSED MEANING

The reversed meaning of the Empress card speaks to us of feeling worthless, putting others first, and generally not valuing ourselves in the way we deserve. You may feel insecure and be neglecting your connection with your feminine side. This is an invitation to get back in touch with yourself and self-worth.

4. THE EMPEROR

This card is related to the element fire and the sign of Aries. It's considered arcana 4, and represents masculine energy (understood in a traditional way), self-righteousness, the father figure, and traditional structures. It also speaks to materialism, earthly possessions, and personal and professional achievements.

When interpreting it, we must consider not only the meaning of the card but also that of the cards surrounding it in the spread and how they relate to one another.

UPRIGHT MEANING

In a spread, we may be dealing with an authority figure (either male or female). This person has a dominating energy, a status of power, and authority based on their material possessions or the place they occupy in a project, in a company, or in society. It's also a card that invites us to be firm and confident when making decisions, and speaks of security and self-esteem in ourselves and in certain situations. In love, it speaks of a relationship where there is a bond linked to sex and the material plane, rather than an emotional connection. In work, it's a good card related to authority and security.

REVERSED MEANING

The inverted meaning of the Emperor card emphasizes the negative facet of all this: arrogance, excessive control, tendency to be domineering and unempathetic. It's an indicator that we could be acting too impulsively and should put more emphasis on being calm and using reason, seeking a balance between our rational and emotional sides.

5. THE HIEROPHANT

This card is related to the element earth and to the sign of Taurus. It's considered arcana 5.

The Hierophant or Pope (depending on the tarot we use) is the male counterpart of the High Priestess. The Hierophant speaks to us of our values, morals, and ethics.

When interpreting it, we must consider not only the meaning of the card but also that of the cards surrounding it in the spread and how they relate to one another.

UPRIGHT MEANING

In a spread, it indicates a situation where we will likely have to decide if something is good, or perhaps some kind of situation where we may have to consider moral and ethical issues. This card invites us to look for the answer in ourselves, to take into account traditional values or practices, to realize that by transcending them we can find a universal truth. If we're asking for someone, it speaks of a person who is very much a spiritual person with very high moral values. In love, it speaks of empathy and a traditional relationship. In work, it speaks of trusting those with professional experience and giving value to teachers.

REVERSED MEANING

In general, this reversed card speaks to us of having doubts about what is right, or being involved in a situation that may not be beneficial on a spiritual or moral level for us or others. It's also related to challenging the established power, going against the rules, and rebellion.

6. THE LOVERS

This card is related to the element air and to the sign of Gemini. However, it can also be related to the earth element.

The Lovers speaks to romantic love, but also to relationships between people in general, about friendships and things we have in common with other people.

When interpreting it, we must consider not only the meaning of the card but also that of the cards surrounding it in the spread and how they relate to one another.

UPRIGHT MEANING

This card speaks to us of relationships between people. In this sense, it has a positive connotation. In these relationships, or rapport, communication flows and there is an attunement between the feelings and affection of both people. We can also interpret it in a more literal sense: a romantic relationship, a wedding, or the process of falling in love. In love, it is obviously one of the best cards we can find, and although it can speak of a strong bond, it usually refers to the early stages of a relationship. In work, it invites us to focus on relationships with others, to concentrate on communicating and creating a work team, not doing it all by ourselves.

REVERSED MEANING

The reversed meaning of the Lovers card speaks of an imbalance in our emotional relationships, a frustration at not knowing how to relate, or a problem with our partner; it may be a communication issue, not having the same type of interests or feelings, or couple problems in general. In this position, this card invites us to seek the reestablishment of balance in our relationships through communication.

7. THE CHARIOT

This card is related to the element fire and the Sun or the planet Mars, although it's also related to the sign of Cancer.

The Chariot is usually a positive card, but it depends on the context. It can give us a "yes" to our question, progress, strength, and encouragement to achieve what we desire. Victory is in our hands.

When interpreting it, we must consider not only the meaning of the card but also that of the cards surrounding it in the spread and how they relate to one another.

The Chariot

UPRIGHT MEANING

In a spread, it indicates that we are in a moment where events are happening quickly, that we are moving forward in the desired direction, that we will be victorious; success is near and we are going to achieve it. In a more literal sense, the Chariot can also signify a trip or move, as well as matters directly related to cars. It can also refer to a change of place in your life (in a more metaphorical way), but always a change that you perceive as positive. In love, it may be a relationship where things are moving too fast or you (or the other party involved) feel that things are moving too fast. It also encourages us to propose or lay our cards on the table. At work, it's related to a time of energy and looking at the long term.

REVERSED MEANING

The reversed meaning of the card speaks to us of not being in control of the situation in which we live, of feeling that we are not in control of the aspect of life that worries us. The card invites us not to look for culprits but to let ourselves flow and not try to control everything.

8. STRENGTH

This card is related to the element fire and to the sign of Leo. It is considered arcana number 8.

The card of Strength speaks to us of inner strength and virtues related to it: determination, security, peace, and control over oneself, one's body, and one's emotions. Traditionally, it's represented by a woman opening the jaws of a lion.

When interpreting it, we must consider not only the meaning of the card but also that of the cards surrounding it in the spread and how they relate to one another.

UPRIGHT MEANING

When the Strength card appears in a tarot spread in an upright position (facing us), it speaks to us of a situation or someone with a strong will, courage, patience, balance between body and mind, and usually luck. They're seen as a person who does well precisely because of their work and self-control. Your mind should control your body and your impulses, not the other way around. Whether in love or at work, this is a good situation, a strong and safe moment that we may be going through (or will go through).

REVERSED MEANING

The reversed meaning of the Strength card speaks to us of a lack of control over ourselves: We may be succumbing to laziness or impatience. In general, it relates to a lack of control over our emotions and our mind. The card recommends we get back in touch with ourselves, get back on the ground, and slowly work on our security and find some order.

9. THE HERMIT

This card is related to the element earth and to the sign of Virgo.

The Hermit speaks to us of wisdom, experience, and the need for silence and solitude in order to know ourselves. It's a card whose fundamental theme is the spiritual quest.

When interpreting it, we must consider not only the meaning of the card but also that of the cards surrounding it in the spread and how they relate to one another.

The Hermit

UPRIGHT MEANING

The Hermit speaks to us of a journey, a spiritual quest, in the company of oneself, of introspection and the deep meaning of life. The Hermit invites us to seek personal fulfillment in the spiritual, in our inner selves, and in our self-knowledge, and not so much in earthly pleasures or immediate gratifications. It may indicate a period of loneliness. It will certainly show a search for a meaning beyond the obvious. In love, the Hermit card can speak of a significant relationship, or the search for a more serene and mature love. In work, the card invites us to focus on rigor and study.

REVERSED MEANING

The reversed meaning of the Hermit card may have to do with feelings of isolation, loneliness, and helplessness. It may indicate that you need a break or isolation for a while, or it may be that you have entered a loop of isolation that is not beneficial to you and you need to stop.

10. THE WHEEL OF FORTUNE

This card is related to the element earth and the planet Jupiter, which is the traditional ruler of fortune and good luck. It's considered arcana 10.

The Wheel of Fortune, more than a stroke of good luck, speaks about the unexpected, about the twists and turns that life takes, and teaches us that sometimes you are on top and then, suddenly, you are at the bottom.

When interpreting it, we must consider not only the meaning of the card but also that of the cards surrounding it in the spread and how they relate to one another.

The Wheel of Fortune

UPRIGHT MEANING

The Wheel of Fortune speaks of a moment in time where things can change and destiny has something unforeseen in store for us. It may also want to speak to us about being prudent with ostentation or pride, because one day things can go well and the next they can go terribly wrong, or the other way around—things change suddenly, for better or for worse. In other cases, however, it can also speak of good luck or a stroke of fate in our plans. Often it's best to let go and assume that life is often cyclical and changing. In questions where we seek a definitive answer (especially when we are looking for a "yes" or "no"), this card does not want to give us a definite answer. Both in work and in love, the Wheel of Fortune encourages us to enjoy it; if we are not in a good moment, it encourages us to remember that no evil lasts forever. It invites us to assume that nothing is eternal, neither the good nor the bad.

REVERSED MEANING

The reversed meaning of the card speaks of a period of "bad luck." The lesson the card provides us with in this position is that sometimes life does not give us what we want, but we have no choice but to move forward and see what unexpected paths open up before us.

11. JUSTICE

This card is related to the element air; to the sign of Libra, which is represented by a scale; and to its ruler, the planet Venus.

Justice, in addition to being able to speak to us about legal matters, refers to balance, equilibrium, equanimity, and honesty.

When interpreting it, we must consider not only the meaning of the card but also that of the cards surrounding it in the spread and how they relate to one another.

UPRIGHT MEANING

In a spread, it indicates that the process in which we are involved will not have a quick resolution; it will be slow because this is a very static card. It recommends we follow the rules, do things right, have a good head on our shoulders, and trust that when the time is right, the result will be positive for us, if we have done things the right way. If our question is related to making a decision, this card invites us to decide according to what is true and fair, without hidden interests or lies. In love, it's a positive card signaling that, if we have established a good foundation of honesty and trust, things will flow. At work, it recommends that we act in an equal, fair, and balanced way. If we are asking about someone, the card speaks of a fair and clear person.

REVERSED MEANING

The reversed meaning of the Justice card makes us see that we may be in a situation of imbalance or injustice. We may be paying the consequences of our actions or other people's actions, but there will be a situation that we will perceive as unjust or as "karma" toward us or the person we are asking about; there is a lesson to be learned in this regard.

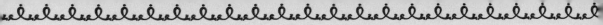

12. THE HANGED MAN

This card is related to the element air and is considered arcana 12.

The Hanged Man is not an accurate name, since the card is intended to actually reflect a situation where you're suspended in the air and a bit in limbo; in no case does it have to do with a hanging or punishment of any kind.

When interpreting it, we must consider not only the meaning of the card but also that of the cards surrounding it in the spread and how they relate to one another.

UPRIGHT MEANING

In a spread, it indicates a situation at a standstill, where we're frozen in time or in a moment of our life. In that frozen-in-time moment, we are in an uncomfortable, new, or challenging position where we aren't totally at ease, where we do not know if the role we're playing is the right one. But this has a very positive side. This challenging role allows us to see things with a new focus and point of view, broadening our horizons and giving us a new vision of who we are or what we're doing. It also shows us that we may be in a situation where we feel unable to make a change, trapped and sacrificing ourselves for the sake of others. The invitation is to try to see things from another perspective so we can know what direction to take, taking advantage of the unique circumstance we are in. In love and work, it can make us see that we feel somewhat stagnant or in a circumstance where we can use that to our advantage by approaching things from another angle.

REVERSED MEANING

In a reversed sense, the card of the Hanged Man can make us see, on the one hand, that we believe we are right and are observing things as they are, but on the other hand that we are not really looking at things from the viewpoint of the truth, but from our partial and limited vision. We may also feel trapped or bound, with no way out. The invitation, once again, is to embrace the discomfort and try to approach the problem from another angle.

13. DEATH

This card is related to the element water and to the sign of Scorpio and the planet Pluto, both of which are related to the cycles of life, transformation, and change.

The Death card very rarely refers to a literal death. It usually refers to the end of some circumstance or stage (good or bad).

When interpreting it, we must consider not only the meaning of the card but also that of the cards surrounding it in the spread and how they relate to one another.

UPRIGHT MEANING

In a spread, the Death card speaks to us of the end of a cycle and the beginning of a new one. It reminds us that nothing lasts forever, but just as it announces the end of a stage, relationship, or any type of circumstance, it means that, as a result, we're entering a new stage of our life. Normally, it's an unscheduled change that we do not actively choose, but rather we undergo the change. The fundamental message of the card is that we should accept this change as part of life and embrace the new stage that lies ahead of us. In a relationship or job, from the most radical perspective, it could be the end of a chapter, but it could also be the end of a paragraph: a change or end of a stage within the relationship or job itself without necessarily being related to a breakup or dismissal (although it can be).

REVERSED MEANING

The reversed meaning of the Death card is similar to that of the upright card, but with a very important nuance: While in the upright position you receive the change with acceptance, making it easier, in the reversed card the person inquiring will show much resistance to this change, which will mean suffering. The lesson will be to assimilate this card and assume that nothing in life lasts forever, and that an end means a new beginning.

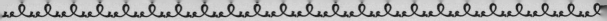

14. TEMPERANCE

This card is related to the element earth and to the sign of Sagittarius (even though it's a fire sign). It's considered arcana 14.

Temperance shows meaning related to that virtue: patience, moderation, equanimity, and tranquility in the face of the hands we are dealt by life. Let yourself flow.

When interpreting it, we must consider not only the meaning of the card but also that of the cards surrounding it in the spread and how they relate to one another.

UPRIGHT MEANING

In a spread, it indicates the virtues of patience and self-control. It transmits the message to us to be equanimous, to be calm and tranquil in the face of a problem. We should let ourselves flow like the water seen in the card, without letting our nerves get to us or losing our heads in the process. It's a card that recommends that we take a middle path, control our emotions and thoughts, and not be radical in the decisions we make but let things rest and decide from a moment of serenity and calm, never agitation. It also speaks of the ability to adapt to circumstances and to others, to be like water. In love, it shows a moment of great peace where you find support and calm in the other person, and it's reciprocal. In work, it indicates that you will maintain tranquility and others will see you as a judicious, calm, and quiet person.

REVERSED MEANING

The reversed meaning of the Temperance card speaks of losing one's temper, tranquility, and serenity and of going through a turbulent moment. The card invites us to distance ourselves, calm down, and make an effort to regain tranquility through an inner quest—although for this we can seek support from others.

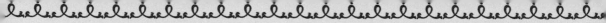

15. THE DEVIL

This card is related to Saturn and Capricorn. Not because Capris are very bad, but because it's a card related to the limits and the chains that we impose on ourselves (and we Capris are pretty much like that; we carry burdens for no reason).

The Devil, therefore, speaks to us on the one hand of self-imposed limitations and, on the other, of problematic actions.

When interpreting it, we must consider not only the meaning of the card but also that of the cards surrounding it in the spread and how they relate to one another.

UPRIGHT MEANING

In a spread, it indicates a situation where we're working against our own long-term benefit because we're basing our well-being on short-term satisfaction. It can speak to us about vices, about sex (especially without intimacy, as something purely physical), and about the chains we put on ourselves without realizing it, about how we're limiting ourselves and making ourselves feel bad for no reason. You may feel like a victim of your circumstances, but the key to changing your situation is in your hands—you just have to realize how powerful you are. It shows us that many times we are victims of our character and weaknesses and we hold the power to work on that. It can speak to us about a relationship that is based on sex and the physical, or one that is somewhat toxic, which we're emotionally attached to. At work, it speaks to us of the one we do not like, but from whom we cannot say goodbye because we feel they're our obligation. In both cases, the card shows us that we have the power to put our foot down and change our destiny.

REVERSED MEANING

The reversed meaning of the card speaks to us of liberation—to get out of a situation where we felt bad, slowly get rid of it, and feel free.

16. THE TOWER

Although at first glance this card can be quite scary, it's not as negative as it may seem, since, like all arcana, it has a lesson to teach.

When interpreting it, we must consider not only the meaning of the card but also that of the cards surrounding it in the spread and how they relate to one another.

The Tower

UPRIGHT MEANING

The Tower is one of the most striking cards (perhaps the most) in a tarot spread. The Tower signals a vital moment, certainly not a simple or pleasant one, a moment of destruction and many changes. It's not showing us something negative that happens one time, but rather an internal process in which we consider many things that we believed to be true and suddenly all those truths fall apart, and life forces us to change. We will rethink who we are in a deep and conscious way. Out of this process a new version of ourselves will emerge, but through a process or circumstance that will force us to destroy our previous version. In love, it's not a positive card, but it can indicate the end of a relationship that deep down was preventing us from evolving and moving to the next level in life or work.

REVERSED MEANING

The reversed meaning of the Tower card is very similar to when it is upright, but in this case it speaks of less dramatic and drastic change. It will be a more subtle transformation, and easy to integrate. You may suffer from fears and insecurities, but deep down you will be aware that the change will be positive.

17. THE STAR

This card is related to the element air and to the sign of Aquarius.

The Star, as shown in the image, speaks of something light, pure, bright, and fortunate. It speaks of a good moment, something magical and good for you or for the person asking or the circumstance you are asking about.

When interpreting it, we must consider not only the meaning of the card but also that of the cards surrounding it in the spread and how they relate to one another.

UPRIGHT MEANING

In a spread, the Star card is one of the best cards we can find; it has practically no negative connotations. This card symbolizes many virtues: inspiration, tranquility, good luck, spirituality. It signals that what you are asking about will turn out well. Your life is guided by your rational mind and accompanied by emotions. In this way, mind and heart go hand in hand, in a fluid, luminous, and natural way. In love, the Star is a great card where illusion and a beautiful and pure relationship that makes you feel good stand out. In work, it means finding something that you are good at, that you enjoy, and where you feel that everything flows.

REVERSED MEANING

The reversed meaning of the Star is not negative; this magnificent and brilliant meaning simply becomes more serene and less spectacular, but it is still positive.

18. THE MOON

This card is related to the element water, the Moon as a star, and the sign of Pisces. In astrology the ruler of Cancer is the Moon, but in tarot, it's related to the sign of the fish.

It speaks of the occult, the mysterious, femininity, intuition, the unconscious, the oneiric, anxiety, and dreams.

When interpreting it, we must consider not only the meaning of the card but also that of the cards surrounding it in the spread and how they relate to one another.

UPRIGHT MEANING

In a spread, it indicates a situation that is suggestive and inspiring, but also unclear, almost unreal, where we feel hopeful that all will turn out okay, but we also feel fears, anxieties, and a kind of sense of unreality: We feel that things are not what they seem. It also invites us to enter the world of the esoteric and the spiritual and to follow our intuition. This card connects us with our feminine, intuitive, fickle, and emotional side. It speaks to us of our feelings and sensations, good and bad, and how we see them reflected in others and project them consciously or unconsciously. Illusions, deceptions, and imagination also play a fundamental role in this dream world where everything seems relative and illusory. It can also speak to us of facts or data that are hidden. In love, it shows insecurities and fears; in work, things that are unclear.

REVERSED MEANING

The reversed meaning of the Moon card symbolizes that we can finally overcome these doubts, fears, and mistrust. It can also tell us that those things that were hidden are finally unveiled and show their true face or meaning.

19. THE SUN

This card is related to the element fire, the Sun as a star, and the energy of Leo.

The Sun is arcana number 19 and symbolizes new beginnings, the luminous, childhood, the secure and visible. It's generally a very positive, encouraging, and happy card.

When interpreting it, we must consider not only the meaning of the card but also that of the cards surrounding it in the spread and how they relate to one another.

The Sun

UPRIGHT MEANING

In a spread, the Sun card shows us a new beginning, from innocence, happiness, and hope. It represents warmth, beautiful relationships with others and with ourselves, and situations in which we feel good and we feel loved, in which our inner child is ebullient. It's usually related to the external, what is in the light, and to the masculine side. In love, it can symbolize a new relationship that excites us, but also the birth of a child or a common project. In work, it can symbolize new opportunities and beneficial situations.

When illustrating my tarot cards, I enjoyed rethinking the patriarchal association between the internal and unclear (the woman, the moon) and the external, safe, and luminous (the man, the sun), so I decided to represent both cards with female figures, to show the virtues of both one and the other from a new point of view.

REVERSED MEANING

The reversed meaning of the Sun card speaks of disillusionment, disappointments, situations that have not met our expectations, being let down in love. Although it has this sadder nuance, it's not a terrible message either, simply something temporary that will soon be in the past.

20. JUDGMENT

This card is related to the element air and, in some traditions, to the sign of Aquarius.

It's considered arcana 20, the second-to-last one of the deck; we are coming to the end of the journey.

Judgment speaks to us of justice, not from an earthly point of view, as in the Justice card, but in the sense of judgment toward ourselves.

When interpreting it, we must consider not only the meaning of the card but also that of the cards surrounding it in the spread and how they relate to one another.

UPRIGHT MEANING

In a spread, the Judgment card invites us to review our internal dialogue, to forgive ourselves for our mistakes, to take care of ourselves, to assume the ultimate consequences of our character, and to value ourselves from a radical point of view. It speaks to a sense of full and consistent personal fulfillment, of coming to peace with our mistakes, the mistakes of others, and all the worldly situations we have to experience, and accepting our lives with grace. This card encourages us to give ourselves courage, to have a healthy relationship with ourselves, and to feel worthy of everything good that we deserve. In love, it indicates a positive time, but based on respect for oneself and acting accordingly. In work, it represents a time of deserved achievements and self-affirmation.

REVERSED MEANING

The reversed meaning of the Judgment card shows us that we have a problem with self-worth, self-esteem, or the relationship we have with ourselves. It invites us to discover how valuable we are and to become aware of all the good we have to offer to the world and to ourselves. Reevaluate your relationship with yourself and begin to love and care for yourself more.

21. THE WORLD

This card is related to the element water, and it's considered arcana 21, with which we conclude our journey.

The World is a card of total openness to life, to the possibilities it offers us when we have already integrated all the arcana and life experiences.

When interpreting it, we must consider not only the meaning of the card but also that of the cards surrounding it in the spread and how they relate to one another.

UPRIGHT MEANING

In a spread, the card of the World speaks to us of totally opening ourselves to life and its possibilities after having integrated the learnings of all the arcana and life experiences. It suggests that we communicate, open up, and enrich ourselves with life experience. It's a very positive card, signaling fullness, celebration, and sharing our happiness with others. From a more superficial point of view, it speaks to us of communications (a call, a WhatsApp message) that we are awaiting and finally receive, of social networks and the media. It's the epitome of what human experience means in its deepest aspect, and it also speaks to us about processes that end satisfactorily. In love, it's a good card, symbolizing a relationship in which we reach our purest potential and unselfishly surrender. In work, it shows professional fulfillment, the achievement of goals and desires.

REVERSED MEANING

The reversed meaning of the World card indicates unresolved issues or stages, which are unfinished and generate frustration and sadness. Your efforts seem to be useless and you feel stagnant, but this card in this position invites you to not give up and instead keep going, because it does not represent a definitive no but rather a call for hope.

Two of Cups

MINOR ARCANA

Interpreting the message of the majors

Although the minor arcana are also complex and worthy of study, here's a summary of what these cards mean. You can start working with them once you have an understanding of the meaning and archetypes of the major arcana. In my tarot, the Tarot de Carlotydes, each suit follows a chromatic range, based on color theory, to make interpretation easier. In addition, each suit is inspired by the folkloric tradition and idiosyncrasies of a different people.

	SWORDS (AIR, REASON)	WANDS (FIRE, CREATION)	CUPS (WATER, EMOTION)	PENTACLES (EARTH, MATERIAL)
ACE (POTENTIAL)	Power, clarity, victory	Creation, inspiration, strength	Intimacy, well-being	Prosperity
TWO (DUALITY)	Choice, dichotomy	Discovery, new adventures	Attraction, partnership, union	Adaptability, balance
THREE (COMMUNICATION)	Pain, grief, heartbreak	Preparation	Community, friendship	Collaboration
FOUR (STABILITY)	Recovery, rest, pause	Celebration, party	Apathy	Security
FIVE (ADVERSITY)	Tension, problem, discussion	Misunderstanding, dispute	Loss, repentance	Poverty, worries
SIX (GROWTH)	Transition, travel	Progress, self-esteem	Nostalgia, innocence, childhood	Charity, generosity
SEVEN (FAITH)	Disappointment, betrayal	Perseverance, competition	Fantasy, illusion	Investment, vision
EIGHT (CHANGES)	Loneliness	Changes, movement	Evasion, deception	Commitment, training
NINE (RESULTS)	Despair, anxiety	Perseverance	Satisfaction	Luxury, gratitude
TEN (EPITOME)	Loss, crisis, pain	Responsibility	Happiness	Wealth, status
ELEVEN (ACTION, MESSAGE)	Curiosity	Enthusiastic	Affectionate	Entrepreneur
HORSE (MOVEMENT)	Argumentative, sharp	Passionate	Romantic, charming	Efficient
QUEEN (INFLUENCE)	Perceptive, rational, cold	Exuberant	Empathetic, intuitive	Loving, attached
KING (AUTHORITY)	Intellectual, clear thinking	Visionary, courageous	Emotionally balanced	Controlling, disciplined

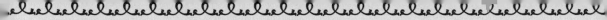

Nine of Gold

THROWING THE CARDS

SHUFFLING

There are different methods for shuffling cards. Some artists say that it should always be done in the same direction or with the same hand. In my opinion, let your intuition guide you, and shuffle them well while thinking about your question.

THE SPREADS: What and how to ask?

You can ask the tarot for a spread without thinking of a specific question. That spread will provide you with information about the person consulting the cards, and from there, you can probe further into what has come up in the spread or ask more specific questions.

There are infinite layouts and types of tarot spreads. In the following pages you'll find some of my favorites. However, you can create your own tarot spreads, or draw cards intuitively and place them on the deck in order.

Six of Wands

Four of Swords

If you're just starting out, it's best to draw a few cards at first and gradually incorporate more complex spreads to see how cards relate to each other.

Writing down your interpretations of different card combinations in your tarot journal will allow you to see what resonates with you—this will enable you to continue to learn and improve.

You can start by throwing the cards for a friend or acquaintance and gradually go deeper into this world.

DIFFERENCE BETWEEN TAROT AND ORACLE

The tarot always follows the structure we have just discussed. The oracle is a freer type of deck, without rules, where the artist chooses the meaning of each card and there are no archetypes.

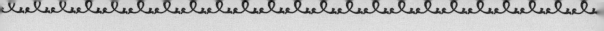

I   2   3

SPREAD 1:

For asking advice about
a problem.

1. Your problem.
2. How it affects you.
3. How to overcome it.

SPREAD 2:

For simple love.

1. Relationships in general.
2. What the person feels.
3. What the other person feels.
4. What will happen.

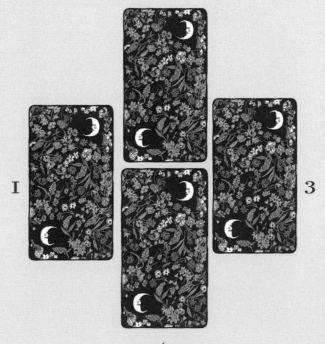

SPREAD 3:

To know if a person thinks about you.

1. How you are with that person.
2. How you feel.
3. How that person is with you.
4. What that person feels.
5. Future situation.

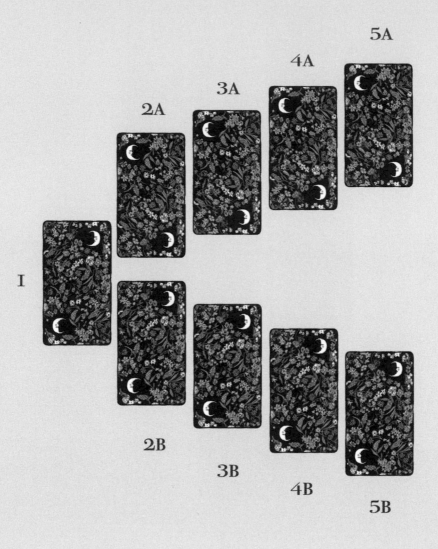

SPREAD 4:

To know what happens depending on whether you do something.

1. Current situation.
A. If I do that.
B. If I don't.

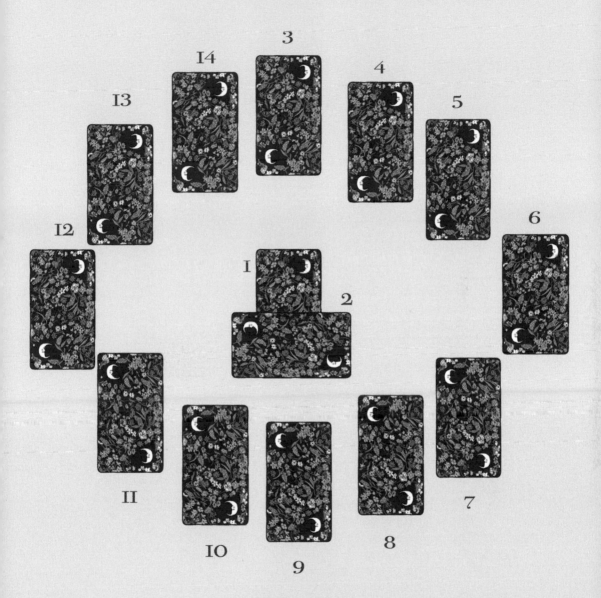

SPREAD 5:

To know how the following year will go (the energy of each month).

1. The energy of the year.

2. The challenge of the year.

3–14. The energy of each month in chronological order
(3 corresponds to January, 14 to December).

CRYSTAL BALL

Aside from being a popular association with witches, the crystal ball is one of the oldest means of divination to see visions of the past, present, and future. To learn how to use it properly, it's necessary to practice a lot and be consistent.

1. Clean and activate your crystal ball.

2. Observe it in the twilight with the light of a candle behind you.

3. If you manage to focus your attention, you will begin to see somewhat blurry images. Write down what you see in your grimoire or in a notebook you use only for this purpose.

4. Never leave the ball uncovered or in the sunlight.

PENDULUM

The pendulum is a divination tool consisting of a quartz hanging from a small string or chain. It's used by swinging it over a small board or paper that says "Yes," "No," and "Maybe."

To use it you must connect to it—clean and activate it like the rest of your magic items.

It's a very powerful tool for simple questions. To use it, hold the pendulum above the board and let it swing freely, while you hold steady, making no movements.

RUNES

Runes are small pieces of wood or other carved material. There are several types of runes; the best known are the Viking runes, of Scandinavian origin. To use them, besides cleaning and activating them, you must know the meaning of each piece and throw them on a board to interpret which ones fall and how they do so. Here is the general meaning of each rune to serve as a guide.

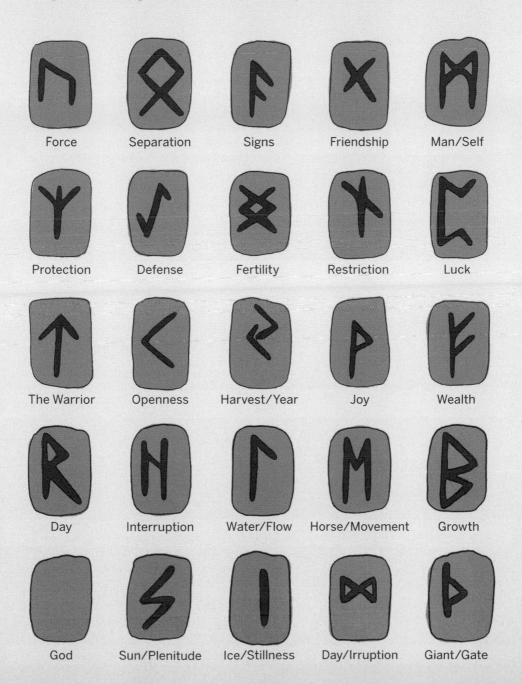

Force	Separation	Signs	Friendship	Man/Self
Protection	Defense	Fertility	Restriction	Luck
The Warrior	Openness	Harvest/Year	Joy	Wealth
Day	Interruption	Water/Flow	Horse/Movement	Growth
God	Sun/Plenitude	Ice/Stillness	Day/Irruption	Giant/Gate

PALM READING

The reading is first done on the right hand,
then contrasted with the information on the left.
The ratio is approximately 80 to 20 percent, respectively.

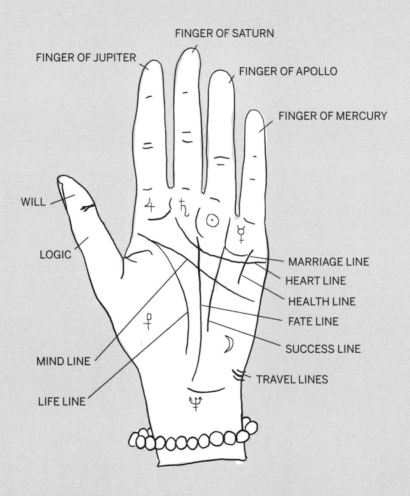

FINGER OF SATURN

FINGER OF JUPITER

FINGER OF APOLLO

FINGER OF MERCURY

WILL

LOGIC

MARRIAGE LINE

HEART LINE

HEALTH LINE

FATE LINE

SUCCESS LINE

MIND LINE

TRAVEL LINES

LIFE LINE

The intersections and divisions of the lines should be observed. The astrological symbols indicate the different mounts that are related to their planetary rulers and the themes they occupy in other disciplines such as astrology. The prominence of these mounts is also an aspect worth analyzing; the most voluminous ones are the most relevant areas. These are the main lines, but there are other more partial aspects to interpret.

TASSEOMANCY (OR READING TEA LEAVES)

This is the intuitive reading of the tea leaves after drinking a cup of tea. There are also other techniques with coffee. This is a general guide.

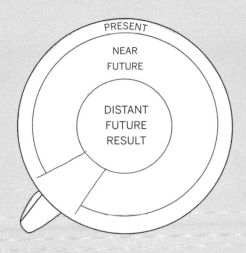

PRESENT

NEAR FUTURE

DISTANT FUTURE RESULT

Bad health   Decisions   Bad news

Good health   Luck   Good news

Travel   Business   Problems

Visit   Efforts with no results   News (neutral)

CEROMANCY

(See chapter 3 for information about candles and ceromancy.)

OUIJA

The Ouija consists of a board with letters, numbers, and a "yes" and a "no." It emerged in the nineteenth century when spiritualism became fashionable. In the sessions, contact with deceased people is made. The participants put a finger on a glass placed facedown on the board, the spirit is invoked to give answers, and then the session is closed by thanking the spirit. From a spiritual point of view, it's a practice that many consider dangerous and not advisable because we cannot be sure that we are contacting the desired person, since another entity may impersonate them. From a scientific point of view, the glass moves because the participants, unconsciously, move it.

10.

MAGICAL RECIPES AND RITUALS

- Witch Salts
- Florida Water
- Cascarilla
- Protection Spray
- Seven Knots Binding
- Spells in a Jar
- Amulets
- Familiars
- Love Rituals
- Abundance Rituals
- Protection Rituals
- Manifestation

WITCH SALTS

Salts in magic are generally used for protection and as an ingredient in protection rituals. There are different types, with various nuances to their use. These salts should not be ingested; they're for magical works and rituals.

pink salt • red salt • purple salt • black salt • table salt • sea salt

Himalayan pink salt: It's a natural salt with a pinkish hue. It protects relationships and love bonds. It removes negative energy and blockages.

Red salt: This is not a naturally occurring salt; it's made with sea salt, paprika, pepper, and red coloring (optional). Set an intention while making this salt. The intention should be related to love, romance, passion, sex, and pleasure. Together with black salt, red salt can also be used for turning and other protection rituals.

Purple salt: This is sea salt with lavender and violets (purple coloring can also be added). It's a softer protective salt that provides tranquility and serenity.

Black salt: Also known as the "witch salt," this is the most potent of all. It's the most powerful for protection, cleansing, and banishing rituals. To make it you will need to be patient, as it is a laborious process. There are many experienced craftspeople who make it, so you can buy it directly from your trusted witch, but if you want to make it yourself you will need:

- A cauldron or deep casserole dish
- Burning coal
- Cinnamon sticks
- Clove
- Dried rosemary
- Sea salt

To promote self-protection, burn all the ingredients except the salt, until they are completely reduced to black ashes. Mix with the salt and store in a dark place.

(Some recipes include ashes and burned matches; I prefer to make it with the above ingredients.)

Table salt: It's protective, gentle against bad energies, and cleansing.

Sea salt: This salt helps balance emotions, cleanse, and protect.

Magic trick: To protect a room with salt, do an energy cleanse, then throw a few grains of black or sea salt in each corner of the room.

FLORIDA WATER

Agua Florida, or Florida water, is a cologne with citrus and cinnamon notes to which magical properties are attributed. Its origin dates back to the nineteenth century, in the United States, and although the first and most famous commercial brand of Florida water is Murray and Lanman, you can make this tonic at home. A multitude of magical properties are attributed to it: energy cleanser, attractor of abundance, and good luck. After cleaning my space, I finish with a sprinkle of Florida water.

FLORIDA WATER

YOU WILL NEED

- 2 lidded glass jars of at least 2 liters (2 quarts) capacity, sanitized
- 1 orange
- 1 tangerine
- 1 lemon
- At least 1 liter (1 quart) of full moon distilled water

- 2 cinnamon sticks
- Cloves
- Fresh lavender
- Fresh rosemary
- 1 tablespoon ground dried mint
- 96% alcohol, such as moonshine or vodka

METHOD

- Peel the fruits and cut the skin into small pieces.
- Add half of the distilled water to a jar.
- Place the fruit skins in the jar.
- Add the cinnamon, breaking it with your fingers a little to release more scent, and the cloves.
- Add the herbs (first break them up a little with your fingers).
- Fill the jar halfway with the alcohol then add the remaining distilled water so that everything is covered.
- Close the jar and shake.
- Let stand at least 14 days away from sunlight.
- After that time, filter the mixture with a cloth and a funnel and pour the cologne into another jar.

CASCARILLA

The cascarilla is a magical element and its fundamental function is to protect. It's very common in Caribbean magic. It involves grinding eggshells (which naturally have a protective function in nature) in your mortar until they're completely reduced to a white powder. Leave the powder to charge in the light of the full moon in a glass jar without a stopper. To store, keep in a dry, dark place with the lid on.

PROTECTION SPRAY

You can prepare this spray with different protective elements (see the correspondences throughout the book). Here's the recipe I use after cleansing my space to "seal" the energy cleanse, or before meditating or performing a ritual.

YOU WILL NEED

- Amethyst
- White quartz
- Sage or rosemary
- Sea salt
- Full moon water
- 3 drops of patchouli essential oil
- 3 drops of lavender essential oil

METHOD

Place all the ingredients in a lidded glass jar or atomizer, and mix well.

SEVEN KNOTS BINDING

A binding is a very powerful spell to attract something or someone to your life. In no case should it be done to bind a person to love you, because you are conditioning their willpower and that will bring misfortune to both you and the person you bind. But we can use this layout as a spell to attract what we want (abundance, for example).

The following is one of the most famous and powerful bindings, the so-called seven knots binding.

ELEMENTS
An 8- or 28-inch red cord that should be touched only by the person making it.

WHEN?
During a full moon.

By the knot of one, my spell has begun (set intention).

By the knot of two, it will come true.

By the knot of three, so it will be.

By the knot of four, this power is stored.

By the knot of five, my spell is alive.

By the knot of six, my future I will decide.

By the knot of seven, events grow.

SPELL OR KNOT TYING
Then the knots are undone to release the power of the spell in this way: one knot per day consecutively and in the order in which they were tied (from one to seven) to release the energy, so that the last one you tied is the last one you untie.

SPELLS IN A JAR

These are short rituals in which we introduce elements in glass jars with a certain intention. We can carry them with us as an amulet, give them as a gift, or leave them in a space with an intention. They are kept as long as we deem necessary, then they are buried to return them to nature. All spells in a jar are sealed with candle wax of a color corresponding to the intention, and before starting they're cleaned with a lighted incense stick that is briefly introduced inside.

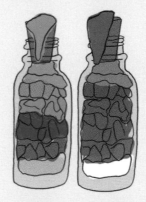

SPELL FOR SELF-LOVE OR ATTRACTING LOVE

Himalayan pink salt, rose quartz, red jasper, basil, lavender, honey, rose petals, hibiscus, and pink wax.

SPELL TO ATTRACT HAPPINESS AND HARMONY

Sea salt, basil, citrine, carnelian, sunflower seeds, rosemary, and yellow wax.

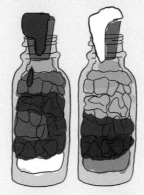

SPELL TO EMPOWER INTUITION

Sea salt, amethyst, labradorite, cinnamon, cocoa, rose petals, and purple wax.

SPELL TO CONCENTRATE AND STUDY

Himalayan pink salt, red jasper, amethyst, rose petals, lavender, and white wax.

SPELL FOR ECONOMY AND ABUNDANCE

Rice, mint, 3 drops of patchouli essential oil, ground cinnamon, a bay leaf, sigil of abundance, and green wax.

PROTECTION SPELL

Black salt, tourmaline, white sage, onyx, rosemary, protection sigil, and black wax.

AMULETS

Amulets are objects that people wear to protect their energy. They are usually elements that exert a double protective and aesthetic function, such as pendants or bracelets. Here are some of the most common and my favorites. We can also have our own amulets of protection and good luck, objects that simply have a special meaning for us.

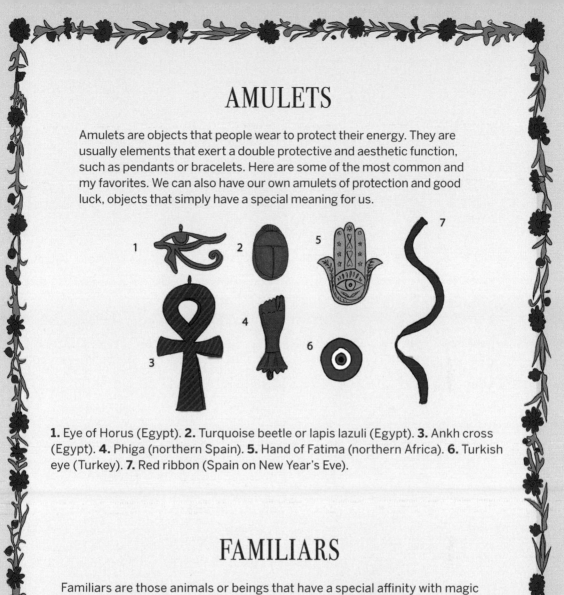

1. Eye of Horus (Egypt). **2.** Turquoise beetle or lapis lazuli (Egypt). **3.** Ankh cross (Egypt). **4.** Phiga (northern Spain). **5.** Hand of Fatima (northern Africa). **6.** Turkish eye (Turkey). **7.** Red ribbon (Spain on New Year's Eve).

FAMILIARS

Familiars are those animals or beings that have a special affinity with magic and a very close bond with their owner or human familiar.

It's very common for familiars to be pets, but not all pets are familiars.

Some traditions also consider other beings, many of them mythological, to be familiars, such as fairies or gnomes, as well as spiritual or nonmaterial beings.

LOVE RITUALS

Love rituals can be used to improve our relationship with ourselves (self-esteem, self-worth) and to improve our relationship with another person (sweetening). A sweetening is not a binding; it is used to improve harmony in a relationship, whatever it may be; it is white magic. A binding is a very complicated work of black magic, which consists of dominating the will of one person to be with another. It can have very strong adverse effects for both people involved and is often difficult to reverse.

For this reason, in these pages you will find love rituals, a ritual to attract and find love, and a ritual to sweeten a relationship (not necessarily romantic), but in no case a binding.

SELF-LOVE RITUAL TO INCREASE YOUR ATTRACTIVENESS: APHRODITE BATH

The ritual consists of preparing on your altar some bath salts inspired by the goddess Aphrodite and taking a ritual bath on a full moon with the purpose of increasing self-confidence and self-love and attracting more "suitors" (as my grandmother would say) or being more attractive. If you don't have a bathtub, you can fill a bottle of water, mix it with the salts, and rinse yourself with it in the shower. After a ritual bath or shower, do not rinse with running water until the next day; just pat dry with a towel, without dragging it along your body.

YOU WILL NEED

- Himalayan pink salt

- 3 drops of rose hip oil

- Rose petals (if possible, fresh; if not, dried petals are also fine)

- 1 tablespoon dried lavender

- 1 teaspoon sugar

METHOD

In a lidded glass jar, mix the salt, rose hip oil, rose petals, lavender, and sugar. Light a pink or white candle during the ritual.

RITUAL TO ATTRACT LOVE

This ritual comes from the spell book of my friend's mother who met the man who is now her fiancé the day after performing it. I do not guarantee that the results will be so immediate, but if what you really want is to find love (besides focusing on yourself, working on self-love, etc.), I suggest you perform this ritual.

YOU WILL NEED

- Full moon water (can be from another moon)
- Honey
- Cardamom
- Cinnamon

Timing: sunrise, crescent or full moon

METHOD

Boil moon water in a saucepan with honey to taste. Add the cardamom, then add the cinnamon. Let the infusion cool and drink it slowly. When you leave the house the first time after doing the ritual, go out with your dominant foot first (the right one if you are right-handed) and say, "I am ready for the universe to send me a person with whom to feel good and calm, in love and happy."

SWEETENING RITUAL

This ritual serves to improve any type of relationship (partner, family, friend), enhancing the positive parts of the relationship and making it easier to understand each other.

YOU WILL NEED

- A small pink candle
- A piece of white paper and a red pen
- A white plate

- Honey
- Sugar
- Cinnamon

Timing: crescent moon

METHOD

Light the pink candle, and set your intention to sweeten the situation. Write the person's name three times on the paper. Fold the paper and place it on the plate. Pour the honey, sugar, and cinnamon onto the paper. Meditate on your intention. When the candle is extinguished, bury it all.

ABUNDANCE RITUALS

Abundance is not only economic prosperity and material goods but it's also feeling content and peaceful. It's important to work on feeling abundant and deserving of attracting money and economic stability to our lives. Here is a very simple ritual to attract abundance and material prosperity to your home, and another one to attract opportunities and open the paths that were closed (not only in the workplace) due to an energy blockage.

CINNAMON RITUAL

Done on the first of each month, this is one of the most effective and simple rituals for attracting abundance and economic resources to your life.

YOU WILL NEED

- 1 tablespoon ground cinnamon

METHOD

Put some cinnamon in your right hand on the first day of the month. Stand at the threshold of your home (at the front door), facing the inside of your house. Close your eyes and say or think, "This cinnamon will attract abundance to this house." Blow the cinnamon from your hand (remember, facing inward) and do not sweep or wipe the entrance until the next day.

ROAD-OPENING RITUAL

This ritual is designed to break energy blocks that limit opportunities we naturally attract with our energy. With this ritual you perform an energy cleanse of yourself and the space on a waning moon and also do a physical cleaning of your home: Throw away what you don't use, objects or gifts from people who are no longer in your life, and those things that do not transmit good energy, and air it out well.

There are many types of rituals that are called *road openers*. Here's one that is very simple and effective.

YOU WILL NEED
- Palo santo or rosemary incense
- 1 purple and 1 gold candle
- Pencil and paper
- 1 cloth bag (preferably gold)
- Key
- 3 coins
- Matches

Timing: on a full moon

METHOD
- Do the cleanse (energy and physical) on page 190.
- Light the incense in your magical space, let it burn out completely, and light another one to begin the ritual.
- Set intentions for the candles:
  - Purple candle (used to transmute energy): With a needle or athame carve, "Transmute the negative energy and unblock."
  - Golden candle: Carve the word that best represents your purpose (abundance, money, strength).
- Write on the paper a short letter to the universe to ask for help unblocking the situation that is troubling you and say thank you.
- Fold the paper once, and put it in the bag with the key and coins. Leave the bag next to the candles while they burn out.
- Light the golden candle, and wait for it to burn out on its own. Light the purple candle when the golden one is consumed. While it burns, pass the incense through the rooms of your house.
- When the candles have burned out, put a drop of wax from each candle into the bag.
- Put the bag in a drawer where no one will touch it and keep it there until things improve.
- When you feel that the situation has been unblocked, bury the bag in a garden or pot, once again giving thanks.

PROTECTION RITUALS

A protection ritual is a magical process that prevents negative energy from interfering in our rituals and in our life in general. As we have seen, one of the best ways to protect ourselves is to do an energy cleanse and wear an amulet (or have it in our magical space). But there are times when it is necessary to take more drastic measures to protect ourselves energetically, not to do harm, but to prevent others from doing it to us.

THE PHIGA

As shown earlier, the phiga is an amulet, but it's also a gesture (page 187) that can be used to protect us when we enter a place or situation where we feel that the energy is not the best, or to protect us from someone who wishes us harm.

FREEZING

The act of eliminating a person from your life by writing his or her name on a piece of paper and putting it in a glass in the freezer is called "freezing a person." This is very drastic and should not be done lightly, only as a last resort. It's better to protect ourselves energetically and try to avoid being affected by the negative energy that others project on us.

TURNING

The turning ritual consists of returning negative energy to the person who wishes us harm or who has done some magical work against us. It's a very powerful ritual intended simply to return the energy, not to harm. Therefore, if the person has not wished us any harm or done anything to us, we have nothing to fear.

YOU WILL NEED

Matches, 1 white candle, and 7 black candles

Timing: new moon

METHOD

We place on our altar the white candle and around it the 7 black candles in a circle. The white candle represents us, and the black candles represent the person, persons, or negative emotions that may exist against us. We light the white candle while holding the thought that it is a representation of us, and we light each black candle while concentrating our energy and saying to ourselves, "The evil that this person has wished us, may it be returned seven times." It's important that it is seven times, because this way the ritual will be more powerful. Ideally, if it has worked, our white candle will still be lit before the black ones are consumed. It's important to analyze and interpret the remains of the wax, which candle is extinguished last, and how the ritual develops in general.

LOSING FEELINGS FOR A PERSON

Although it doesn't have to be considered a protection exactly, a very useful ritual that my friends often ask me about is one to leave behind a past love, turn the page, or stop having feelings for a person with whom we cannot be or who has hurt us. One way would be to regularly use the Aphrodite salts discussed on page 188, to gain self-esteem and self-love, but if we want to do something more radical yet simple, we can try to accelerate the healing process with this ritual.

YOU WILL NEED
White thread, 2 white candles, a pin or athame, and matches

Timing: on a waning moon

METHOD
Prepare yourself and your magical space, and then write your name on one of the candles and the name of the person you want to stop having feelings for on the other candle. In this way, the candles will be a representation of each of you. Then tie them together with the thread. This union symbolizes the relationship you had and the feelings that tie you to that person.

Light a match and visualize how the fire will destroy that bond. Light your candle and then the other person's candle. Observe how they burn and how at a certain point the thread burns and the bond will be broken.

Now interpret these aspects: the fire of which candle broke the thread, whether it takes them a short or long time to burn and be consumed, and what the wax residue looks like. In this way you can see how strong the bond is and who is still hanging on to the other person to a greater or lesser extent.

Once the ritual is finished, dispose of the remains away from your home.

QUICK PROTECTION RITUALS

Create a vision: Imagine yourself inside a sphere where only positive energy can reach you and negative energy bounces away from you. Spend a couple of minutes a day thinking about it and feeling it.

Find a quiet place in your home, in your magical space, or in nature. Stand up straight, close your eyes, and breathe deeply. Visualize how your body fills with golden light; feel how this light protects you and gives you confidence.

Charge a black stone (onyx, tourmaline, obsidian) in the light of the full moon, set an intention on it with the idea of protecting yourself, and try to always carry it with you (a good option is to choose a small stone or wear it in a pendant, ring, or bracelet).

MANIFESTATION

Manifestation is a technique to attract into our lives those things we believe we deserve, want, and value. To do this, we must vibrate from abundance, being grateful and complete with what we have in the present moment, but visualizing ourselves with those things we long for and projecting how we feel with those things, as if they were already in our lives. The best times to manifest are full moons and energetic portals with synchronistic numbers, such as 2/2/22 or the days of August 8 or November 11, as they are respectively 8/8 and 11/11 and therefore very powerful energetic portals. However, like everything in magic, we can manifest when we feel it is right and it resonates with us.

There are many methods to manifest, although the key to everything is what I have described in the previous paragraph. Here is one method of manifestation:

- Light a white candle with a match on a full moon, if possible by the light of the moon itself.

- Connect with yourself, breathe consciously, and relax. Manifesting is closely linked to spirituality and the universe; you must take the time you need to set aside for a moment your most superficial concerns.

- Write on a white paper those desires you have as if you already have them. That is, do not write "I want to have more money" but "I attract the money I need," "I have everything I need," "I am a source of abundance." Always keep it positive and write it in the way that most resonates with you.

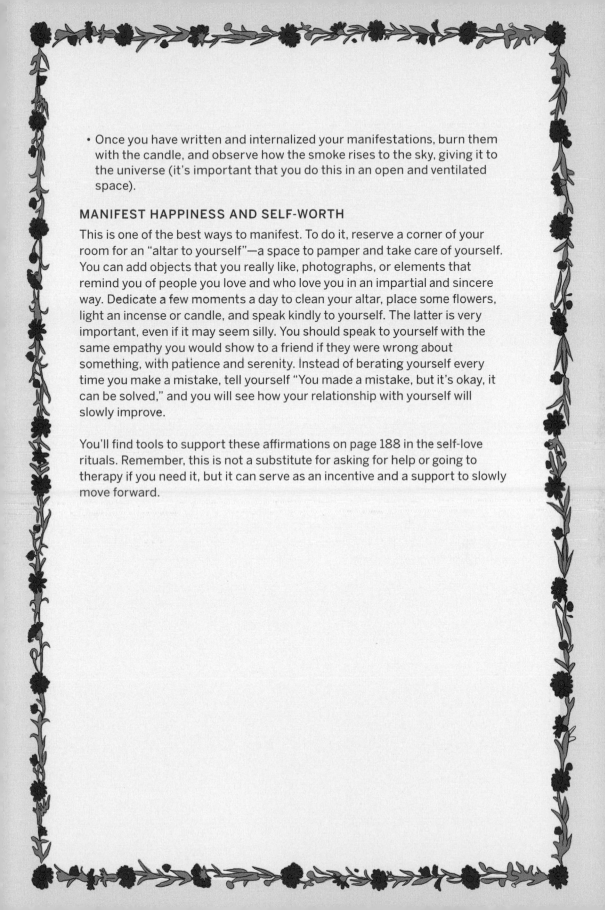

- Once you have written and internalized your manifestations, burn them with the candle, and observe how the smoke rises to the sky, giving it to the universe (it's important that you do this in an open and ventilated space).

MANIFEST HAPPINESS AND SELF-WORTH

This is one of the best ways to manifest. To do it, reserve a corner of your room for an "altar to yourself"—a space to pamper and take care of yourself. You can add objects that you really like, photographs, or elements that remind you of people you love and who love you in an impartial and sincere way. Dedicate a few moments a day to clean your altar, place some flowers, light an incense or candle, and speak kindly to yourself. The latter is very important, even if it may seem silly. You should speak to yourself with the same empathy you would show to a friend if they were wrong about something, with patience and serenity. Instead of berating yourself every time you make a mistake, tell yourself "You made a mistake, but it's okay, it can be solved," and you will see how your relationship with yourself will slowly improve.

You'll find tools to support these affirmations on page 188 in the self-love rituals. Remember, this is not a substitute for asking for help or going to therapy if you need it, but it can serve as an incentive and a support to slowly move forward.

To sum it up,
the magic world is
quite extensive, but I hope
I've managed to clear the way
for you in this wonderful world so
that you can find yourself, spend
some time exploring yourself,
and investigate everything
that is not immediately
obvious to you. I hope you
find your own way of
being magical.

Acknowledgments

Thank you to my loved ones for all their support and affection
and for providing me with a welcoming environment where I can be
myself and do things from the heart, like this book.

To my mother, for making me feel safe, protected, and loved,
as well as giving me the opportunity to discover the magic of art,
mythology, and film from a very young age, and thus expanding
my horizons, my creativity, and my awareness.

To my grandmother Rosa, for teaching me the value of
being independent, hardworking, and, above all, generous.

To my grandfather Lesmes, for his generosity and sensitivity;
I miss how he always managed to surprise me with his opinions
and ideas.

To my father, for teaching me the value of hard work and
the ability to always see the positive side of situations
and people (something I'm still working on).

And finally, to all the girls and women who have ever been told
that they are too sensitive or too intense. May they learn to see
that therein lies their strength and their greatest power.

Carlota

About the Author

Carlota Santos is the author of *Signs of the Zodiac* and an illustrator living in Spain. In 2020, she began to share drawings on Instagram as @carlotydes on topics related to astrology, from her own perspective and with a touch of humor. Currently, with thousands of followers around the globe, Carlota Santos is a vibrant and unique voice in the astrology universe, teaching the subject matter in a visual way.